PRAISE FOR

TO LOVE AND BE LOVED

"What does it mean to be a loving person? If you want to answer that question and start along that path, this is the perfect guidebook—rich in metaphor, deep in meaning, and beautifully written." —JAMES A. AUTRY, author of *Love & Profit* and *Confessions of an Accidental Businessman*

"Over the millennia, the Great Masters have revealed to us that every cell in the human body is filled with love. Sam Keen's stirring odyssey of love takes this microscopic truth to its most complete expression." —T. C. McLUHAN, author of *The Way of the Earth* and *Cathedrals of the Spirit*

"A persuasive case for the practice of loving oneself and those around us in a manner that is deep, true, and satisfying. Using personal narrative and stories told to him by students and friends, Keen maps out scenarios and solutions, writing in a quietly elegant voice that calmly reminds us of that which we were born knowing: that we were born to love."
—*Sonoma County Independent*

"Sam Keen delivers another insight-filled bull's-eye with *To Love and Be Loved*, a charmingly honest, no-holds-barred examination of that bittersweet fact of life many try to deny: 'amo ergo sum' (loosely translated, 'to live is to love')."
—*NAPRA ReView*

"The most valuable gift in Keen's book is its vision of a greater love, a vast, all-inclusive, personal and impersonal love that can take us beyond self and relationship to participate in the nature of God." —*Lotus/Personal Transformation*

TO
LOVE
and
BE LOVED

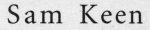

Sam Keen

BANTAM BOOKS
New York   Toronto   London   Sydney   Auckland

This edition contains the complete text of the original hardcover.
NOT ONE WORD HAS BEEN OMITTED.

TO LOVE AND BE LOVED

A Bantam Book
PUBLISHING HISTORY
Bantam hardcover edition published August 1997
Bantam trade edition / May 1999

Grateful acknowledgment is made for permission to reprint the following:

Excerpt from "East Coker" in *Four Quartets*, copyright © 1943 by T.S. Eliot and renewed 1971 by Esme Valerie Eliot. Reprinted by permission of Harcourt Brace & Company.

Excerpt from "For the Time Being," by W. H. Auden. From *W. H. Auden: Collected Poems*, by W. H. Auden, edited by Edward Mendelson. Copyright © 1944 and renewed 1972 by W. H. Auden. Reprinted by permission of Random House, Inc.

Every reasonable effort has been made to trace the owners of copyright materials in this book, but in some instances this has proven impossible. The author and publisher will be glad to receive information leading to more complete acknowledgment in subsequent printings of the book, and in the meantime extend their apologies for any omissions.

Library of Congress Catalog Card Number: 95-52610

ISBN 0-553-37528-8

Published simultaneously in the United States and Canada

Bantam Books are published by Bantam Books, a division of Random House, Inc. Its trademark, consisting of the words "Bantam Books" and the portrayal of a rooster, is Registered in U.S. Patent and Trademark Office and in other countries. Marca Registrada. Bantam Books, 1540 Broadway, New York, New York 10036.

PRINTED IN THE UNITED STATES OF AMERICA

BVG   10 9 8 7 6 5 4 3 2 1

To Norman and Lyn Lear and the Gulley Gang,
one and all seasoned in the great arts of conversation,
companionship, and compassion.

In *quantum physics*
as in love,
in searching out
matter and meaning
paradox rules.

Protons, being particle and wave,
persons, being single and connected,
arrive at their destination
before they embark on the journey.

The arrow of longing
hits the target
before we take aim.

The answer sleeps
in the question.

The lost treasure
is our found/ation.

Start with the conclusion,
the end encoded in the beginning.

The problem of the meaning of life
is solved by the mystery of love.

CONTENTS

PART I
Becoming a Lover: The Great Art

PART II
The Elements of Love

PART III
Meditation on Faith, Hope, and Love

I

BECOMING A LOVER:
THE GREAT ART

LOVE AND
THE MEANING OF LIFE

~~✕~~

*Love is the ideal of all of us; intimacy and mutually elevating
equality, complete trust and maximum esteem, for both ourselves
and others. . . . Who can say: "I don't want to love" or "I
can't love," without the most profound regrets?*
—ROBERT SOLOMON, *THE PASSIONS*

A letter from a 42-year-old woman whom I do not know
states the matter with painful clarity: "I can't find any meaning
in my life. I feel ashamed to admit it, but I have never loved or
been loved by anybody except my parents. No husband, no
lovers, no friends."

In the depths of our being, in body, mind, and spirit, we
know we are created to love and be loved. Fulfilling this imperative, responding to this vocation, is the central meaning of
our life.

Our first and last visceral certainty is that we are safe and
satisfied only when we are encompassed by loving arms and
that we flourish only within the ambience of adoring eyes
and shared joy. We long for tacit knowledge, for soft caresses,
lips on lips, skin gliding along skin. In the once-upon-a-time of
childhood and in the fullness of our sexual maturity, we find

respite from fear and suffering in that sanctuary we create when contoured bodies cuddle quietly or entwine in passionate love. In our declining years, when death has claimed our companions, the ache of loneliness is healed only by the balm of touch. Our eyes continually venture forth to play with other eyes, flirting, caressing, hoping to see and be seen. Our minds come alive and grow strong in the give-and-take of muscular conversation, dancing and wrestling with ideas. And when we dare to dream of a dwelling place that might satisfy our deepest longings, we imagine a community founded on justice and ruled by compassion and kindness.

The sad news is that we frequently know about the necessity for love because of the void and violence created when we were ignored, injured, abused, abandoned, or betrayed by those who loved us unwisely or not at all. Nothing dramatizes the necessity and centrality of love in human life more than its absence. To the degree that we are haunted by feelings of abandonment, loneliness, emptiness, and the meaninglessness of life, we know we *ought* to have loved and been loved better by our parents, our neighbors, our friends, our mates, our children. Our outrage and inrage testify that we are furious because we have been denied our birthright. Our shame and sense of embarrassment are evidence that we have not been looked upon by loving and accepting eyes. At the dead end of our addiction to booze, cocaine, sex, or "the bitch goddess of success," we always discover that what we were blindly running after was love and that all we ever caught was a poor substitute. And it didn't satisfy us because we can never get enough of what we didn't want in the first place.

The glad tiding is that our quest for love is nevertheless perennial and ineradicable. We can fail and fail, but just when we are tempted to despair, some blind impulse impels us to take another run at glory. The gospel of the possibility of love seems to be built into human nature.

In the deepest recesses of our imaginations, we cherish the hope that love is finally grounded in ultimate reality. This hope often remains hidden because it is an embarrassment to our modern minds. On the evening news we watch the growing anarchy of nations, the resurgence of genocide, the rising tide of refugees, and the population explosion, and we lean toward despair. But probe beneath the secular surface, and you will find a spiritual intuition alive and well—but shy. In the face of the tragedy and suffering of human history, we, with Einstein, refuse to believe that "God plays dice with the world." We continue to hope that, as Martin Luther King, Jr., preached, "unarmed truth and unconditional love will have the final word in reality."

If we allow this hope for the final triumph of love (not knowing what it might be), we do so because we believe, with Pascal, that "the heart has reasons the mind knows not of." When it comes to calculating the power and reach of love, the mind is a pedestrian but the heart is a broad jumper. The spirit leaps the chasm of despair in a single bound to entertain the possibility that love is the force that moves the cosmos, the energy that creates a marriage of hard rock and swirling water, that keeps the stars on their courses, that stirs me to procreate a child who, quite unknown to my dying self, will carry the imprint of my days into history.

Love is all this and more. And the nearer we get to it, the more we know we have come home. It is where we came from and return to, the before and after that we approach in our best moments. It is the source of life, the meeting place of our origin and destination. In those moments when love finds us, we lose one identity and gain another. We burst out of the dark cocoon of the ego and discover that we have grown wings.

It is easy for a cynical mind to dismiss the intuition that we are made to love and the hope that unconditional love will have the final word as a matched pair of illusions. After all, the news of most any day suggests that what makes the world go round is not love but fear, greed, competition, cruelty, and the will to power.

But if modern psychology has taught us anything, it is that conscious appearance is often the opposite of unconscious reality. The overt and unquestionable fact that we frequently act in thoughtless, selfish, and cruel ways is *not* conclusive evidence that we are essentially brutish or that we have no intuition of the centrality of love. That we lie does not prove that we do not know the truth.

To the contrary.

Human beings are the only animals capable of self-deception and therefore of self-betrayal. The first human invention was language; the second was lying. Our minds, hearts, and psyches are split screens. We are weird amphibians, simultaneously inhabiting solid knowledge and liquid illusion. We play a game of hide-and-seek with ourselves in which we are both hider and seeker. In dreams we are the knower of multiple hidden truths, the censor who decrees that such forbidden knowledge can be revealed only in bizarre symbols, and the waking self to whom the dream is addressed. At one and the same time, we know the truth and hide it from ourselves; we simultaneously cultivate illusion and conspire to disillusion ourselves.

The paradox of love that I want to understand was stated by the early atomic physicist who said, "I have my solutions, but I don't know how to arrive at them."

This is the Great Puzzle that confronts us all. Something stops us from laying claim to the heartland, the homeland we have never left. Why do we hide from ourselves? Why don't we apply the knowledge we have about love and meaning? Why isn't love the cloud that guides us by day and the pillar of fire by night? Why do we own a castle and live in a shack? Why do we study war and not love?

Better yet: Why do *I* hide from myself? What keeps *me* from

6

being more animated by my intuitive knowledge that love is the way, the truth, and the life?

Love's Illusions: *Bad Advice from Dr. Lonelyhearts*

Ultimately, the persistence of hatred is part of the mystery of evil that the philosopher Karl Jaspers called "the rock on which every system of philosophy shipwrecks." It is easy enough to see that unloving and abusive parents produce children who are likely to pass on the habit of lovelessness generation after generation. It is equally clear that most societies encourage cooperation and communal affection among their members but promote suspicion and hatred of outsiders.

I can offer no final explanations for why we idealize love so much and practice it so little. Or for that matter why, against all odds, kindness sometimes springs up in conditions that seem destined to produce only cruelty. What I can promise is to dispel an enormous amount of the false mystification that surrounds our ideas of love.

It is passing strange how poorly we think about love. In matters amorous, our minds turn to mush.

For openers, consider the lopsided amount of attention we have paid to the definition, measurement, and cultivation of intelligence, in contrast to our failure to investigate the many modes of love. We have a national obsession with IQ, but we never seriously consider the possibility that we possess an LQ, a love quotient, a genetic aptitude for empathy or compassion that may be enhanced or diminished by circumstances.

Without doubt we desire love, dream about it, are disappointed by its absence, and become angry when it vanishes. In fact, love has become the secular equivalent of the Holy Grail—the magic treasure that should save us. But we *think* about love, if at all, as a kind of warm, squishy, pink feeling like the grace of God or a chinook wind that is supposed to come mysteriously out of nowhere and bring eternal spring into our frigid hearts. Unless and until that happens, we wait, and wait for Godot, the godlet that might bring happiness to our strife-filled lives. It seldom occurs to us that while we wait, we might analyze the complexities of love and figure out how to *do it*.

Amazingly, many books about love complain that we can't understand love because of the poverty of the English language. We "love" ice cream, our mothers, and our mates indiscriminately. Supposedly other tongues are richer. Ancient Greek had *agape*—the godly, altruistic, self-giving concern for the downtrodden that is so praised in the New Testament; *eros*, the hungry desire to possess the other; and *philia*, the brotherly love that is as rare in Philadelphia as it was in Athens. French has *l'amour*, which is superior to English *love* because it is done by Frenchmen and -women.

The fault, however, lies not in our language but in our laziness. We crowd into one simple word *love* a host of feelings and sensibilities that should be distinguished and mapped.

Turn with me to number 887 in that great hymnal of language—Roget's *Thesaurus*. There under *love* you will find an English vocabulary that is more than adequate to express the nuances of *agape, eros, libido, caritas, amour*, and all the kaleidoscope of love. You will find gentle affections and virtues: *sweet charity, cherishing, protection, kindness, tenderness, benevolence, sympathy, fellow-feeling, understanding, fondness, liking*. And all the urgent impulses that impel us into flirtatiousness, romance, and seduction —the *yearning, mutual attraction, fascination, enchantment*, and *bewitchment* that may lead us in the way of passion or prurience. Our language allows us, in the name of love, to span the distance between dalliance and commitment, lust and adoration, obsession and compassion.

The problem we have with love is not an inadequate vocabulary. In fact, the availability of such a stunning variety of words to express all of the nuances of love that we systematically ignore is a symptom of our dis-ease. As Erich Fromm said in the midcentury classic *The Art of Loving*, "In spite of the deep-seated craving for love, almost everything else is considered to be more important than love: success, prestige, money, power—almost all our energy is used for the learning of how to achieve these aims, and almost none to learn the art of loving."

Today it is even clearer that we misunderstand love because we have chosen to worship power and security; we fail in compassion because we have become obsessed with actualizing our individual potential and increasing the standard of living for those within the closed circle of our own hearth; we silence the reasons of the heart because we have chosen to follow a path of heartless knowledge; we do not adore because we insist that every thing and person be of use; we do not care because we have come to believe that it profits a man or woman well above the prime rate to trade the soul for a piece of the action.

There is, of course, one variety of love that occupies the center of our attention. *The contemporary imagination is fixated on Intimacy, the Deity of Love that is manifest in the triune form of Sex, Romance, and Marriage.* My best educated guess is that fully ninety-five percent of all references to love that appear in the modern media are focused on the promise and problems of romantic "relationships," dyads—the man-woman thing, the woman-woman thing, or the man-man thing. (What the old preacher called heing and sheing, or heing and heing, sheing and sheing.) It is certainly not news to anybody that from the cornfields of Madison County to the lofts of SoHo, romance is alive and flourishing. Yesterday's readers of *True Romance* have become today's consumers of the endless day- and prime-time television soap opera dramas of true and false love. *Playboy* and *Cosmopolitan*, *Teen* and *New Age* are filled with odes to and prescriptions for intimacy. Pop psychology offers advice to the lovelorn. The demand for news from the realm of Aphrodite is constant and insatiable. Endless polls, questionnaires, and research into our erotic habits bolster our questionable belief that we are learning new techniques and making progress in the love game.

In our new mythology, life, liberty, and the pursuit of happiness culminate in dyadic love. If Karl Marx and Marshall McLuhan were alive today, they might issue a joint press release proclaiming that romance and technology (the odd marriage of high-touch and high-tech) have replaced religion as the opiate of the masses.

It is not surprising that popular culture thrives on the romantic myth. What is more disturbing is that there is so little in-depth reflection about the nature of love in contemporary psychology and philosophy. A strange blindness seems to afflict our "seers" and social scientists. For example, without batting an eye, the editors of *The Psychology of Love* and the author of *A Natural History of Love*, two books whose titles would seem to promise a wide-angle vision of the nature and types of love, limit their inquiry to dyadic coupling and ignore most of the varieties of love that have enriched human life through the ages.

And what remedies, what love medicines, are we offered to cure the dis-ease that afflicts our relationships?

A baffling variety! A host of modern authorities, specialists, shamans, and sexperts give us conflicting advice about romantic health. The situation is not unlike the contradictory recommendations for the optimum diet. Dueling scientists and diet gurus recommend that we eat/don't eat meat, margarine, or anything that does or does not cause cancer when fed to a laboratory rat in sufficient quantities. The result is confusion. When it comes to matters of the heart, to how, when, where, whom, and why we should love, we have no warning labels, no committees, no watchdog agencies that evaluate the various therapies offered us by our self-appointed love doctors. Let the buyer beware!

One group that identifies themselves as evolutionary psychologists or sociobiologists offers a problem without a solution, a diagnosis without a remedy. They contend that a hidden evolutionary logic of love and lust predisposes women and men to romantic incompatibility. We are gene-crossed lovers, conditioned by evolutionary history to adopt opposite sexual strategies. As Robert Wright wrote in *Psychology Today*, "If you want to understand the emotional spigots that turn on the attractions, passions, the infatuations that course through you, it helps to think of yourself as a gene machine with a single-minded evolutionary past. . . . Men, at heart, are quantity creatures; women go for quality." It is to men's evolutionary advantage to sow their seeds as broadly as possible, so "they will have sex with just about anything that moves, given an easy chance." It is to a woman's evolutionary advantage to produce and nourish a superior child, so she will choose a mate with the best and brightest genes. Since we are puppets moved by blind evolutionary forces, our "thinking" about sex and romance is done unconsciously by natural selection. The best we can do is to become conscious of the forces that are manipulating us and try to exert some moral force to ameliorate them.

At the opposite end of the spectrum is the growing tendency to see the man-woman thing as a royal path to spiritual fulfillment. Jungian psychologists and New Age gurus view relationship as a sacred journey taken by soul mates whose struggles create a crucible in which each finds a way to completion and wholeness. Pilgrims on this path must take a heroic journey into the depths of their past to discover where they are still ruled by expectations and wounds from childhood, where they superimpose the imprint of their parents on their mates. Remembering the past allows them to reframe their present and reprogram their future. Then the secrets of Tao and Tantra can convert the bedroom into a temple where soul mates explore peak loving, transcendence, and higher consciousness.

Our most popular psycho-erotic experts offer communication as the nostrum for our ills. The problem is that we just don't speak the same language. Since men are from Mars and women are from Venus, we are star-crossed, warriors and lovers, destined to misunderstand each other. Women, we are told, want to talk about their feelings and problems, and men just want to solve them. Women want relationship, and men need to maintain autonomy. We suffer from different communication strategies, tongues, languages. The remedy? Nonjudgmental listening. Encourage your partner to express feelings, and share thoughts by keeping eye contact and giving positive feedback, et cetera.

Inevitably, our culture produces earnest advocates for technological solutions to the problems of intimacy. With profitable regularity the back pages of *The New York Times* and *Playboy* contain advertisements that promise to "put the sizzle back in your sex life" or reveal the secret of sexual power. Your satisfaction is guaranteed if you learn the sexually explicit lovemaking techniques demonstrated for you by experienced couples in full-living-color videos.

Even our most hardheaded specialists reduce love to chemistry—and not of the "moon in June" kind. Listen up to the latest report on the state of the art from the March 1994 issue of *Modern Maturity:*

Chemical attraction. Love: It's all in your mind. Science divides love into two types of chemical behavior. The first comes with infatuation: According to Helen Fisher, Ph.D., author of *Anatomy of Love* (W. W. Norton), it's triggered by a "brain bath" of adrenaline-like neurochemicals. Once the initial rush wanes (usually after two or three years), many people go off looking for it again, becoming veritable "love junkies." For those who stick around, however, there's another type of chemical reward created by a new brain bath of endorphins. According to Mark Goulston, M.D., professor of psychiatry at the University of California at Los Angeles, "Adrenaline-based love is all about ourselves—we like being in love. With endorphins, we like loving."

It is not clear exactly how we are to put such knowledge to good use. Meditating on the matter I was inspired (?) to compose the following:

SCIENTIFICALLY RESPONSIBLE, POLITICALLY CORRECT
PRENUPTIAL DISCLAIMER

Thus, my love,
I pledge my troth:

You must remember this
a kiss won't stay a kiss
a sigh won't stay a sigh
as time goes by . . .

In one short year, or maybe three,
love's brain-bath alchemy
will adrenaline to endorphins turn,
and I for you will cease to burn.

This sweet chemistry of desire
will fade and spark no fire.
So ask not love to be our savior.
It's just a bit of chemical behavior.

Now don't get me wrong. I'm not against intimacy, romance, sex, or relationships between dyads of any gender. We should learn all we can about the evolution of sexuality, our genetic legacy, our gender biases, the nuts and bolts of sexual arousal, and the advanced techniques of Tantric Buddhism. Back in the semidark ages, when I was a neophyte just about to be initiated into marriage, I was given a copy of the then-classic *Ideal Marriage* by Theodore Van de Velde. Therein I was introduced to the mysteries of lubrication, friction, rhythm, positions, and so on. I was taught that it was my duty as a man to learn patience and develop my skill so that I could produce simultaneous orgasms. I was, further, led to understand that oral sex was normal so long as it culminated in intercourse and that coitus interruptus was not a reliable method of birth control. Years later I came across *The Joy of Sex*. I am also in favor of better communication, greater understanding between the sexes, and living happily ever after—with a little help from his and her marriage counselors. I am myself a veteran of analysis Freudian, Jungian, and Gestalt, of Rolfing and various kinds of singles, group, and couples therapy, in which I have learned a thing or two. I am an advocate of marriage, the husband of one practicing wife, the father of three, the grandfather of one.

What troubles me is not that we are so interested in coupling but that we are so uninterested in the other varieties of love that might give our lives greater meaning and dignity.

Our narrow focus on romantic and dyadic intimacy warps our field of vision and produces a severe erotic astigmatism that distorts everything we see and choose not to see. What wonders might our eyes behold if they were not fascinated by, riveted to, a single object of love? Seeing only the good, we blind ourselves to the better and the best.

I fear that many of our popular love doctors are infecting the public with what the radical Catholic philosopher Ivan Illich called iatrogenic diseases—physician-caused illnesses. The ways we think and do not think about love have several regrettable consequences.

First, our obsessive focus on intimacy heightens individualism and creates a form of egotism-à-deux, a style of alienated coupling in which we increasingly neglect the wider sphere within which we need to practice love—the family, the neighborhood, the polis, the land, the wilderness, the community of nonhuman sentient beings. *The terrible mistake of modern theories of love is to focus on two solitary individuals who join together to form an island in an alien sea of anonymous others and unknown neighbors.* The romantic myth is an integral component of the pathological individualism that has become a major threat to Western culture.

Classical philosophers and theologians, the therapists of earlier ages, insisted that love can thrive only in combination with other virtues. For the Buddha, compassion was necessarily linked to wisdom. For Saint Paul, the trinity was faith, hope, and love. For Paul Tillich, love, power, and justice stand or fall together. Most premodern theories consider love to be an elixir that gradually dissolves the boundaries we erect between the self and others and progressively drives the ego beyond individualism, beyond the sanctuary of intimacy, into a more and more inclusive community.

Second, our myopic fixation on romance and sex encourages false mystification, a "fatal attraction" theory, that turns us into victims who "fall" into love due to some mysterious chemistry and fall out or fail to find love because of bad luck, childhood abuse, or "dysfunctional families." This fixation fosters a vain hope that erotic lightning will strike us from heaven and spontaneously give juice and meaning to our lives.

Granted, there is enchantment and mystery in most forms of love—a superrational element, an attraction that escapes analysis. Romance aside, parents love their children in different measure. And who has not found a friend whom one loves more than a brother or sister? Nevertheless, this supercharged element of superfluous affection plays only a minor role in the overall drama of love. Or if it becomes the central element, we remain addicted to romance, victims of the whim of sentiment, never developing a responsible and potent love. Those who perpetually await Cupid's arrow forge no link between love and will.

Third, when we focus obsessively on romance, the single most irrational, volatile, and often illusory form of love, we fail to consider that love may be an art involving skills that need to be developed and practiced throughout a lifetime. As a consequence, we have no school, no curriculum, that teaches us how to cultivate the disciplines and delights of love that give meaning and depth to our lives. When it comes to love, we are emotional illiterates. We know far more about aggression, competition, and developing willpower.

Further to the point: Because we have adopted intimacy as our one test and model of love, we miss the infinite variety of forms that human love can take. This causes us to fall into the destructive notion that there is one right way of loving. The modern world seems to be obsessed with a mania to standardize everything—including love. Love is always supposed to involve intimacy, self-disclosure, and the verbal expression of feelings. Thus the popular notion that a one-size-fits-all set of communication techniques can be applied with the promise of success by anybody in any situation. If only men would tune in to the language of feelings and women to the language of action, we would automatically become effective parents, passionate lovers, and doting spouses. Clearly, strong-silent types are out of fashion. Farewell, Cary Grant and Clark Gable. Hello, Woody Allen.

I suggest that our modern love doctors probably have it wrong in the same way Tolstoy did when he suggested that all happy families are happy in the same way. It is unhappy families and unhappy love stories that are all the same. They all exhibit the same endlessly repeated, boring pattern of resentment, bickering, withholding, blame, disrespect, inattention, abuse, and so on. Happy families and happy love stories, on the other hand, are all creative and unique. D. H. Lawrence and Frieda were a pair unto themselves, as were Gertrude Stein and Alice B. Toklas and George Burns and Gracie Allen.

Some of the world's great lovers were not even "people people," did not discuss their feelings or relationships, and weren't known to have a main squeeze. The Buddha yearned for and found enlightenment and created a community devoted to universal compassion. Jesus, Meister Eckhart, and Saint Francis sought union with God. John Muir's great love affair was with the wilderness, and we are all the richer for it. Georgia O'Keeffe was probably a testy lady, but she cherished bare bones and shamelessly celebrated the erotic curves of the iris and the rose. Picasso was at best careless with and at worst cruel to the women in his life, but he was pure in his love of form, color, texture, and composition. To this illustrious company I might add a handful of marvelous "old maids" and gracious ladies, the likes of Miss Beach, Miss Iney, and Black Elizabeth, who were fountains pouring forth good works, home-baked cookies, and unlimited love in the neighborhood where I lived as a child.

Finally, the most serious consequence of our preoccupation with the mating game is that it keeps us focused on the wrong question.

A woman writes: "How do I best choose my rightful partner? Do I fall back on the prosaic—common interests, values, lifestyles, goals? In which case knowledge becomes the litmus test.

Or do I allow love to choose me, as the saying goes, and dance the waltz of illusion and disappointment, with desire leading the merry chase?"

This is a heartfelt question, asked in complete sincerity, but it is nevertheless a bear trap. Step into it, and you may lose a leg or two. If I ask "How do I choose my rightful partner?" before I ask "How do I become a loving person?" the result is likely to be a disaster, because I will fail to focus my attention on acquiring the skills necessary for becoming a loving human being. *First* cultivate a life filled with compassion, and passion will be added to it. Search only for a great passion, and you will finally despair of love. To those who have, more will be given.

The first and most important question any person can ask is: How can I become a more loving human being?

The remainder of this book is my attempt to answer this question.

Love Is Not a Spectator Sport: *Confession and Invitation*

> For one human being to love another human being: that is perhaps the most difficult task that has been entrusted to us, the ultimate task, the final test and proof, the work for which all other work is merely preparatory.
>
> —Rainer Maria Rilke

It is often said that authors write about what they most need to learn. In my case this is true. I have been a student of love for a long time, but I still have a country mile to go before graduation.

Thirty years ago. I was a young professor with a fresh Ph.D. and an answer for every question. When my wife became troubled and unhappy, I found a psychotherapist and sent her off to be cured. After a couple of sessions, the therapist suggested that I come in and talk to him. Being an enlightened man—who was, by the way, teaching a course on "The Nature of Love"—I agreed to do anything I could to help her with *her* problem. I had insights, theories, and explanations about how her difficulties were causing problems in our marriage. When I went to consult with the therapist, I explained my wife's failings, indicated that I loved her nevertheless, and suggested ways in which she could be fixed. He looked at me as if I had just landed from outer space and remarked in an offhand manner, "I'm sure you think you love her, but I'm not so sure you do." I left the session convinced that he was a mixed-up man.

The following week my wife returned from her session and announced: "Dr. M. said you were part of the problem. He also said that you not only had some hostility toward me, but that you were angry at your mother and distrustful of women in general." I was so shocked that I left the house and went for a long walk, during which I formulated brilliant refutations that I planned to use when I had an occasion to give the good doctor a piece of my mind. Anxious days later I returned to the therapy chamber, stomach churning, to face my accuser. Midway through the hour I began to feel very sick as I got my first glance into the snake pit of ancient disappointment, anger, fear, and confusion that lay at the bottom of my psyche. My image of myself as a nice and kindly man shattered, and I began the long pilgrimage to become what I had pretended to be.

Twenty years ago. Having been divorced, I was living with a woman with whom I was "madly" in love. One bleak day she left me and ran away with a poet (a bad poet, at that), and I was heartbroken and empty. My happiness vanished as suddenly as it had begun when I fell in love. In the painful vacuum that followed, it occurred to me that I needed to learn to love in a different way, one that would not depend so much on how my romantic partner responded to me. I had to stop my frantic search for a woman who would love me and make me happy, and try to figure out how I could become a lover.

Just last week. On the very day I wrote, wisely enough, "Lovers should respect 'No Trespassing' signs and not violate each other's solitude," I tried to force my wife against her stated intention to talk about some difficulties that *we* (not *she*—that's progress!) had been having. You would think that after such a long apprenticeship, I would have become a master of the amorous arts. Alas, not. In the interest of full disclosure, I feel compelled to confess I am still not a model of generosity, a world-class practitioner of compassion, or a black belt in marital arts. I do not radiate *agape*. In the course of writing this book, I have frequently been embarrassed to discover that I know more *about* love than I put into practice.

Thus, what you will find in this book is not foolproof advice by an expert, not the proven program of a therapist who has saved thousands of relationships, nor the formulas of an enlightened guru who has realized the ultimate unity of Being and Love.

But I declare without apology that in my meanderings I have glimpsed love in its various forms and have succeeded and failed often enough to know that the quest to become a lover is the most hopeful and joyful focus for a human life. What I can, therefore, offer is an exploration of the topography of the heart, a collection of love maps that may help you to find your way to hidden gold, rare gems, plants that heal the disease of despair, and elixirs that dispel the miasma of meaninglessness.

This book may be useful to you if:

- You are a beginner—shy, hopeful, and wondering how to tell the difference between love and fascination and explore romance without getting hurt.

- You are lonely and have never mastered the art of friendship.

- You are no longer willing to settle for a separation between love and sex.

- You are a veteran of combat in the erogenous zones— divorced, twice-burned, disillusioned, sick of the gender wars—beginning to fear that "love is only for the lucky and the strong."

- You long for a community where fathers, mothers, grandparents, and neighbors take delight in raising children and band together to care for each other.

- You are frustrated and depressed by the news of growing anarchy, tribal, ethnic, and national violence, poverty, and ecological destruction and want to help create a politics of compassion.

The method of this book is a braid composed of three strands:

Theory. My working assumption, which I will explore shortly, is that what we call love is more like a rainbow than a single color (say, pink). It is a broad and complex spectrum composed of many simple elements, all of which we must understand if we are to develop a lifelong practice of love.

Stories. Since you the reader and I the author are on this quest together, many of the stories in this book come from my experience of the complexities of love. I have also collected stories from friends, from people who have taken my seminars, and from complete strangers whose conversations I have overheard in restaurants or airplanes. In stories not my own, I have changed certain details to preserve the anonymity of my sources.

Practice. I invite you to explore that strand of your autobiography that reflects your experience of love.

Love is not a spectator sport. There are existential questions that are risky and can be asked authentically only in the first person singular. I can ask "Am *I* free? How can *I* love more? What is the meaning of *my* life?" only if I am willing to have my self-understanding, my worldview, my priorities, my relationships, my values, challenged and changed by what I discover. In the final analysis becoming a loving person is not a matter of philosophical analysis or psychoanalysis. It is only when I am willing to *do* the truth and enact love that I discover the meaning of my life.

Amorous Autobiography: *Charting Your Love Journey*

Throughout this book you will find a great many questions addressed to you. These are questions I first asked myself and later asked of others in seminars and workshops. They have no right or wrong answers. In fact, often they have no answers at all. They are simply invitations to self-awareness that may help you assemble the story of your love life.

Composing an amorous autobiography is a lifetime undertaking. In setting out, the most essential thing to take with you is a sackful of important questions. Each question is a minimap that will help you explore some part of the uncharted wilderness of your experience. As you consider each of the elements of love, ask yourself: "What do I know, what have I experienced, of this element of love? How proficient am I in this aspect of the practice of love?"

You may take the idea of composing an amorous autobiography as literally or loosely as you like. Some of you will find it nothing more than a handy way to reflect on the dilemmas and delights of your present and future love life. Others will want to undertake a systematic reconstruction of their love history.

You might keep a journal, a tape recording, or a computer record of the ideas and questions that seem important and the love stories that belong in your autobiography. And/or ask a friend, a lover, a mate, or a small group to join you in exploring. In preparation for writing this book, I collected photographs from every period of my life, put them in order in a scrapbook, and spent two months recollecting and meditating on what I had learned about love from each important person in my life.

There are several things to keep in mind.

First and foremost, remember that you are unique. Your life is a once-told tale, an unrepeatable drama. No one has the same story to tell as you. No one has your mixture of passion and inhibitions, sensuality and fears, generosity and greed. Nobody has identical erogenous zones or ways of expressing love.

Thus, there can be no single model of the ideal lover, no archetype, no universal path. Because we have different histories, personality types, sensitivities, gifts, and wounds, the practice of loving needs to be tailor-made for each individual. You will find that, for a variety of reasons, you are an excellent practitioner of some aspects of love and are ignorant of others.

Different types of people express love in different ways. The native tongue of love may be: sharing ideas, fixing the washer, sending roses, listening, touching, or providing money for college tuition. There are long-distance and short-distance lovers, those who thrive on solitude and occasional closeness and those who love best when they are engulfed in wall-to-wall intimacy. There are celibate lovers and those who are outrageously carnal, passionate intellectuals and great sensualists. Persons who approach the world primarily through thinking and analysis will express love in a different way from those for whom sensing and feeling are prime. Introverts and extroverts, receptive and aggressive individuals, will naturally specialize in different elements of love. How much duller the diamond would be without its many facets!

The best place to start your autobiographical reflection is here and now, with your present love profile.

- Whom do you love? In what ways?

- By whom are you loved?

- How satisfied or unsatisfied are you with your love life, in the broadest sense of the term?

I have found that most people are, initially, no better at taking an accurate love inventory than I was when I tried to advise my ex-wife's therapist. Most of us begin the journey with a faulty compass, misidentify our location, and set out on a road that turns out to be a cul-de-sac. It is all too human for us to assume that the problem lies elsewhere. I'm okay. You're not okay. Adam blames Eve, and Eve blames the serpent, and we have all been blaming each other ever since. When trouble arises, *we* are certain that we are good and *they* are evil, we are loving and kindly and they are hateful and warlike. If only they would become civil, there would be peace in the valley. If we did not have a deeply ingrained habit of blaming others for our deficiencies and failures, therapists would starve to death and there would be no wars.

At the very beginning and at every step along the way, it is important to be as clear as you can about what unfulfilled longings and unmet needs are driving you.

- What is the nature of the love vacuum in your life?

- Do you feel cheated? Abandoned? Not loved enough?

- What would fill the vacuum—a lover, an animal, a mate, a child, a parent, a friend, God?

As you reflect on your strengths and limitations as a lover, you will inevitably be drawn into your past to recollect memories of the gifts and wounds that shaped your style of loving. There are important reasons why you are the way you are that you must understand if you want to change. Someone raised in an abusive or alcoholic family will have a different set of obstacles to overcome than someone raised in a kindly home or a series of foster homes.

- What style of loving was practiced in your family? What was the vocabulary of love—touch, discipline, food, gifts, nurturing your talents?

- Who loved and was loved by whom?

- What did you learn about bodies, touch, sexuality, by the way in which you were touched or not touched?

- Did you have to give up, hide, or reject anything to purchase love?

- Do you feel you were unloved, ignored, abused?

- How is the past still controlling your present? How did your family's way of loving and not loving shape your present life?

These days many people identify themselves as adult children of abusive parents, as victims of sexual or verbal abuse or co-dependent relationships. Many feel they were emotionally abandoned and only conditionally loved by their parents. In addition there is widespread resentment about the ways we were wounded by the gender roles we inherited. Men were taught that they could earn love only by providing, taking charge, being in control, and protecting women and children; women were taught that they could earn love only by being nurturing, sexy, submissive, and passive. It is increasingly difficult to distinguish between the disappointment in love that shadows all but the most fortunate human beings and genuine failure and abuse. We seem to have turned every grief into a grievance. What is certainly the case is that we were all wounded by receiving too little of the right kind of love from imperfect human beings.

Our hope for healing begins when we understand what has dis-eased us. In the measure that we remain unconscious of our past, we inevitably project our habitual fears and expectations into the future. As the American philosopher George Santayana said, "Those who cannot remember the past are condemned to repeat it." If we do not examine our family myths, script, and dramas, we will, predictably, marry a passive-aggressive girl just like the girl that married dear old Dad, or a violent-abusive man just like the man that married dear old Mom. To heal the wounds of our fathers and mothers and avoid inflicting them on our sons and daughters, we must be aware of our dissatisfactions and have some notion of how we would like to change.

Like sailors who navigate by consulting stars or satellites, we can best chart our love journey by a process that involves triangulation between our present, our past, and our imagined future. In addition to a realistic assessment of our current love relationships and an awareness of how our past has shaped and misshaped us, we need a vision of a more ideal future.

The polestar that will guide you into a more loving future is already shining bright in the night sky of your soul. But to see it, you must accustom your eyes to the fertile darkness you have tried to avoid. Look deeply into your disappointments, examine your heartache, interrogate your longing, probe your loneliness, meditate honestly on the elements of love of which you are still ignorant, and you will discover that the void within you is already filled with the desire for fulfillment. Your yearning itself is an internal guidance system that is moving you to become a lover.

> *Waking, we realize*
> *we were asleep.*
> *Everything but love*
> *is a dream.*

THINKING CLEARLY ABOUT LOVE

When I focus on the question "How can I become a more loving human being?" a wild bunch of interesting questions bursts forth. What is love? How do I define it? How much do I love? How can I measure it? If I discover that I am not a very loving person, is there any way I can increase my capacity as a lover? Is love learnable? Teachable? If so, by whom?

Let's acknowledge, before we go further, that there is something foolish about the idea of defining or measuring love. We don't have a science of amourmetrics. Quantifying the gossamer quality that is said to be like a red, red rose or an itch that can't be scratched, that is said to be the senior partner of faith and hope, would seem to be a fool's errand.

But for a moment let's jump to the end of our story, to the philosophical conclusion that seems to emerge with surprising regularity from those who have explored the heights and depths of love. The great lovers throughout human history have testified that, in the final analysis, we do not define or measure love but are defined and measured by it. The more dedicated we become to the practice of love, the more we come to understand that *it is the poverty or richness of our love that defines our sense of what is real.* We experience the self and the world in radically different ways when we are exiles living in isolation from others and when we are at home within a compassionate community of our kindred. Ultimately, love reveals itself to us as more than a feeling, more than a psychological state, more than a sociological phenomenon, more than a bond that unites separate beings in friendship or sexual ecstasy, family, or community. Whereas René Descartes defined the pivotal certainty of the modern objective-scientific mind with the phrase *Cogito ergo sum* (I think therefore I am), the essence of the spiritual vision has always been *Amo ergo sum* (I love therefore I am). If love is—in some sense that we must try to clarify further—a part of the definition of a human *being,* it will forever evade our efforts to define or measure it. We can never fully understand what under-stands our being. But this is getting too far ahead of our story.

Notwithstanding the impossibility of finally defining and measuring love, it is important to think clearly about love.

Ah, but how do we begin to think clearly about love? It is easier said than done. Love is a greased pig. No sooner do you get a hold on it than it squirms and jiggles and runs away. Try to herd it in a northerly direction, and it goes south by southeast. It doesn't take kindly to pens and definitions. And that is the nature of the beast.

It turns out that none of the fundamental characteristics of human beings can be defined or explained. Like love and greased pigs, the complex mysteries of mind, consciousness, self-consciousness, and freedom can be approached only by indirect means—by analogies and metaphors. The mind is like a computer; consciousness is like seeing; self-consciousness is like observing our self; freedom is like being unbound (or is it "just another word for nothing left to lose"?). And love—what is it like?

Love is like: a red, red rose, a hunger, a warm heart, a pleasure bond, a contract to fulfill mutual needs, a promise, a having and holding, a fire that warms or burns, a mother's milk that nurtures, a grafting of two shoots onto a single root stock, a bewitchment, a falling, an internal, infernal itching that can't be scratched, a way of valuing, a taking of responsibility for another, a willful intent to cherish, an intimate communication, a chemical response to a biological attraction, a positive addiction, et cetera, ad infinitum.

Each of the untold number of analogies and metaphors we use in an effort to capture love, that Houdini of the emotions, gives us a fleeting glimpse of some aspect of the phenomenon before it escapes.

When we say "Love is a gift," we are reminded that sometimes it is simply bestowed on us. When we think this way, we might go so far as to define a good friendship, a good love affair, a good family, or a good society as one in which love is freely given and does not have to be earned or deserved.

When we say we are "swept off our feet" and "head over heels in love," we are reminded that passion may rush in like a tidal wave driven by some earthquake in the briny deep and smash every boat in a well-designed harbor.

When we say that love is "a basic need, a drive or instinct," we are reminded that at the very bottom love is something more than a happy occurrence, something more than an emotion or feeling, something more than a way of acting. In philosophical language the impulse to love is said to be a "vocation" or "calling" that is "ontological"—rooted in the fundamental structure of our being. (Thus Paul Tillich's definition: "Love is the ontological drive toward the reunion of the separated.")

I will make use of these and many more analogies and metaphors in the course of trying to understand love. But there are two metaphors that are central in this book: Love is an art; and the various modes of love are compounds made up of different combinations of simple elements.

I choose the metaphor love-as-art because I am most interested in: those aspects of love that are learnable and may be enhanced by practice; love as an action that is within our power; love as a collection of behaviors and skills we may cultivate throughout a lifetime.

Even though love does occur spontaneously in the wild, it is too precious to be left to chance and needs to be systematically cultivated. Calling it an art shatters the naïve notion that it simply happens from doing what comes naturally. A child may run gracefully or have a gift for music, but to become a great athlete or musician s/he must do wind sprints and five-finger exercises. It may seem that lovers, like trapeze artists, meet effortlessly in midair, but such casual grace has been won by a thousand failures and years of discipline.

We practice any art in order to create a habitual pattern of thinking and feeling that allows us to act "spontaneously" in an excellent manner. If love, sweet love is what the world needs now, it is not the sentimental variety but the carefully crafted exercise of compassion, kindness, and wholehearted and wholeheaded passion.

I use as metaphor the periodic table of chemical elements to suggest that the different modes of love—romance, marriage, friendship, charity to strangers, the love of parents for their children and children for their parents, the love we have for a work, a place, a cause—are complex compounds formed by slightly different mixtures of fundamental elements.

Just as matter is not divisible into the simple substances of air, fire, earth, and water, so we must go beyond the simplistic divisions of love into *eros, agape, philia,* and *libido* to discover the underlying principles that will allow us to develop a comprehensive art of loving, a lifelong practice.

As I have reflected on the long history of the philosophical and religious discussions and on my own experience of the nature and varieties of love, I have identified sixteen basic elements that are combined in different measures to make up the different modes of love. (Of course, I might have cut the pie into nine slices, or nineteen. Generosity or courage might have been considered basic elements in their own right, and sexuality might have been subsumed under desire or sensuality.)

As is the case when mixing colors, certain elements are necessarily included and excluded in the makeup of the different modes of love. If you want to create green, you *must* mix yellow and blue.

For instance (in order of increasing complexity):

Sexual lust is a blind drive to gratify a biological drive and achieve a sense of power by reducing the other to a body that can be possessed and conquered. It contains few of the elements of love except a small trace of sensual longing and a touch of erotic desire for what the self feels is missing in itself and that it imagines is present in the other.

Romance is compounded of equal parts of attention, erotic longing, sexual desire, and ersatz adoration created by an idealizing imagination. It feeds on images, projections, and illusion, and it flourishes in the absence of real knowledge about the other. It can exist without any realistic commitment. Romance focuses on what is beautiful, interesting, and desirable and usually doesn't involve a great deal of true compassion, repentance, or sacrifice.

Charity is a dispassionate love that involves empathy, compassion, sacrifice, and a commitment to care for strangers about whom we may have little knowledge and to whom we may not be personally attracted in any erotic way. We may not even want to be friends with them.

A *child's love for a parent* is compounded of need, symbiotic feelings, and sensual desire (*à la* Freud). Because a child has not yet differentiated self from parent, it can progress toward fully mutual love only as it grows into adulthood.

A *parent's love for a young child* involves an enormous disparity in knowledge, power, experience, and caring. At its best, parental love combines attention, empathy, compassion, commitment, unconditional acceptance, and all of the other elements in appropriate measure, including sensual delight and echoes of sexual desire. But sexual expression is absolutely taboo because incest destroys the innocence that is the sine qua non of childhood.

Friendship, philia, involves a full measure of all of the elements except sexual expression. If friends become lovers, the fundamental nature of friendship is changed by introducing a Dionysian, chaotic, and passional element.

A good marriage (legal or otherwise) is probably the only relationship that involves all the elements of love.

At this contentious moment in the history of male-female relationships, it is important for us to note that there is not one set of elements for men and another for women. Society has wounded and rewarded men and women differently. But when it comes to practicing the art and discipline of love, we are equally challenged.

My hope is that you and I may become skillful in forming the many-splendored compounds that will make our lives rich in affection, friendship, charity, protection, kindness, tenderness, benevolence, mutual attraction, sympathy, fellow-feeling, understanding, fondness, liking, fascination, enchantment, bewitchment, yearning, passion, rapture, enthusiasm, flirtatiousness, romance, and all of the other synonyms and varieties of love. If the cosmos could create butterflies and Einstein's mind with a chemistry set that contained hydrogen, oxygen, sodium, and fewer than a gross of other elements, we may be able by mastering the elements of love to perform the alchemy that will change our lives from gross matter to gold.

II

THE ELEMENTS OF LOVE

ATTENTION:
Noticing and Focusing

⌘

Where your attention is, there will your heart be also.
—SANDOR MCNAB

*One day a man of the people said to the Zen Master Ikkyu:
"Master, will you please write me the maxims of highest wisdom?" Ikkyu immediately took his brush and wrote the word,
"Attention." "Is that all?" asked the man. "Will you not add
something more?" Ikkyu then wrote twice running: "Attention.
Attention." "Well," remarked the man rather irritably, "I really
don't see much depth or subtlety in what you have just written."
Then Ikkyu wrote the same word three times running: "Atten-
tion. Attention. Attention." Half angered, the man demanded:
"What does the word* attention *mean, anyway?" And Ikkyu
answered gently: "Attention means ATTENTION."*
—WARREN ZIEGLER
WAYS OF INSPIRITING

SCENE: *The First Time Ever I Saw Your Face*

On December 6, 1974, I was conducting a seminar with Joseph
Campbell and Stanley Keleman on "Myth and the Body." As

37

we broke for lunch, someone entered the room. Out of the corner of my eye, I sensed rather than saw a female presence. Turning my head, my attention was captured by straight shoulders, a proud carriage, a long skirt, a long mane and legs, a hawklike but joyful face, hazel eyes, and a flute flung over the back.

Attention: *Captured and Freely Given*

There is no telling what may happen in Act III of a love story. But Act I of all love stories begins, predictably, with the moment when our attention is captured.

Ordinarily, we ignore most of the people with whom we come into contact. Take a stroll down Main Street, and you will notice that the vast number of "persons" you (do not) meet are an anonymous mass of faceless beings who remain in the background of your awareness, largely unnoticed. Theoretically, they are fellow-beings whom you might come to know and cherish, or dislike. But for all you know, they may be mechanically animated androids who have been manufactured by some mad scientist.

In our "normal" state of mind, we go about the business of daily life focusing on practical matters and ignoring the dramas that are taking place around us. We plan the activities of the day, rehearse what we will say or should have said, and sink comfortably into the familiar routines of home, commute, work, and entertainment. Much of the time our eyes are turned inward, as if we were watching old movies, or we are lost in fantasy, worrying about some catastrophe that may happen or anticipating some future happiness. We see the world through the lens of myth, through Mother-colored glasses, through IBM-colored glasses.

Then suddenly, just when we are walking along, minding our own business, out of the blue something reaches out and grabs our attention. In the beginning what attracts us is not a complete person but an attribute, a predicate, a quality, a single datum, a small gift, a minuscule promise of meaning—straight shoulders, proud carriage, a long skirt, long mane and legs, a hawklike but joyful face.

Think of the moment of first contact, the instant when someone burst into your awareness and a love story began.

SCENE. "We had gone to the adoption agency for our final meeting. And there she was—a small girl child with black hair smooth as a weasel, sitting on a large oak bench in the office, her head tilted slightly to one side, her hand covering her mouth to disguise her shy smile—and my heart was captured in the blink of an eye."

SCENE. "One day, just like any other day, I was riding the bus down Market Street, and I glanced up and instantly fell into the blue eyes of a man sitting across from me. Why I don't know, but I was transported to a mountain lake in the Cascades, and when I noticed his large weathered hands with blue veins carrying rivers of rich blood into the wilderness of his arms, I began to imagine his arms were around me and we were sitting beside a fire in a small cabin. As I stood up to leave the bus, he got up too, and when we met on the curb, he asked me as naturally as if we were old friends, 'Would you like to have a cup of coffee with me?' Of course I said yes. And that was the beginning."

Attraction is a cryptic message that takes time to decode. What we first see, smell, touch, hear, taste, is superficial but symbolic, a token of an invisible world of meaning that unfolds slowly. Our first contact with a stranger may be an invitation, a valentine, or a plea for help. Possibly humans, like other animals, send out chemical pheromones. Certainly we are constantly signaling each other, sending nonverbal love notes to whom it may concern that advertise our goods and needs and invite others to pay attention and establish contact.

At first the nature of the attraction is not clear. The tentative locking-in of attention may occur because of either desire or aversion. The charge may be positive or negative. Initially we may not be able to determine whether we desire or dislike the person to whom we are attracted.

Once our attention is captured, a love story develops only if we escalate the contact by a decision to *pay* attention.

Initially, perception is a relatively passive process. A daffodil or a smiling face seizes our attention. We are drawn to a beautiful sunset in the same way that we "fall" for a winsome man or woman. But very quickly we are faced with a decision about where we will invest our consciousness.

Awareness involves willpower and choice. Inevitably I must pay attention to something—baseball, Bach, or Barbara. Consciousness is like a flashlight that I choose to focus in a narrow or diffused beam. Place an ornithologist and a logger in the same forest, and because of their training and carefully cultivated habits, one will see spotted owls and the other will see timber waiting to be harvested. What you see is what you get. What you ignore is what you do not get. In large measure we are responsible for what we see, hear, touch, and smell. Who we become depends on the interplay between our habitual practice of concentrating and ignoring.

The decision to pay attention to someone is the first act of self-limitation, the first sacrifice, the first gift we make in the name of love.

Years ago I attended a seminar with the great family therapist Virginia Satir. My son had been complaining that I never listened to him, so Virginia had us reenact a typical evening at home. I arrived home from work tired and sank into my favorite chair and started to read the paper. Gifford tried to get my attention in many devious ways: throwing a ball so it would land in my lap, arguing with his sister, talking in a loud voice. I continued to ignore him, and he, disappointed, retreated with his feelings hurt. At this point Virginia had us enact a different scenario in which I started reading my paper and Gifford started bugging me. But then, following her instructions, I laid down the paper, called him over, had him sit on my lap, looked at him directly, and said: "Gif, I'm tired and need a few minutes of quiet. If you will leave me alone for ten minutes then I will play with you." Thirty years later both of us still remember this small psychodrama as the moment when we learned to pay full attention to each other.

In the interest of clarifying the nature of love, the lyrics to the old song might be changed to read: "I can't give you anything but attention, baby."

The price of lasting love is continuing to pay attention to a person, a place, or a work that has become familiar. Paying attention is the bedrock opposite of taking for granted, which is a major cause of death of long relationships.

ATTENTION AND WISDOM

Beware of mirages. Do not run or fly away in order to get free; rather dig in the narrow place which has been given you; you will find God there and everything; God does not float on your horizon, he sleeps in your substance. Vanity runs, love digs. If you fly away from yourself, your prison will run with you and will close in because of the wind of your flight; if you go deep down into yourself it will disappear in paradise.

—GUSTAVE THIBON, QUOTED IN
GABRIEL MARCEL, *HOMO VIATOR*

Paying attention is central to both love and wisdom.

Great mystics and wise men, like William Blake, have always claimed that when the doors of perception are cleansed, everything in the world may be seen through the eyes of love. In those special moments when our perception changes from black and white to full living color, when our eyes are opened, our nostrils flare, and our blood pulses, any loved one, any grain of sand, any flower in a crannied wall, may infuse our hearts and minds with a sense of marvel and meaning. The door to the sanctuary of love is never far away and is always open.

Hopeless romantics and chronically dissatisfied spiritual seekers keep looking toward the beyond rather than the here and now for an object worthy of their devotion—the perfect lover or God. By "falling in love" or cultivating "nonordinary states" of "expanded consciousness" (out-of-body experiences and the like), they seek to have peak experiences and "live high on the mountain of love."

The practice of love and wisdom, as I understand it, leads downward rather than upward, into the valley rather than to the mountaintop. The valley path involves paying extraordinary attention to ordinary things, events, persons. The Zen poet Bashō memorializes a single moment of awareness that contains everything:

> *The old pond*
> *A frog jumps in.*
> *Plop!*

To cultivate love, or whole-soul-fulness, we must resist the temptation to be upwardly mobile, to be always on the move, to pull up our roots and fly to the mythic kingdom of Elsewhere.

The meaning of a thing is not different from the thing itself; it is only the thing fully seen. We come to love not by finding a perfect person but by learning to see an imperfect person perfectly.

ATTENTION AND TIME

To pay full attention, you must stop time and become fully present. Every athlete and lover knows that at the peak of concentration, everything shifts into slow motion and the act and the actor become one.

Several years ago, rafting in the Grand Canyon, I decided I would swim through a moderate-sized rapid. I eased myself off the raft, slipped into the current, and was swept along through the pitching and bucking waves so fast that I arrived at the tail end of the rapid disappointed because I seemed to have had no experience of the event. I swam to shore, walked upstream, and swam the rapid again, and again, until I could slow time down, savor the nuances of the turbulent water, and become one with the river.

Love exists in a zone so different from ordinary time (nearer to dalliance than efficiency) that it is said to be "eternal." A lover abandons schedules and becomes fully present in the timeless moment to a child, a friend, a stranger. In giving ourselves in a passionate sexual embrace to our dearest one, or in caring for a suffering stranger who needs our compassion, we escape from the relentless march of measured time that carries us anxiously toward our inevitable conclusion—death.

Consider the reported dissatisfactions with modern lovemaking as koan, a puzzle to be solved. Women voice a common complaint about men as lovers: "They are too fast. Too goal oriented. Too obsessed with performance and orgasms." As a rule, the human female is a skin creature. Her most erogenous zone is her entire body. She wants to be touched all over before anywhere else. She is not as genitally focused as the male. And above all, she is not in a hurry. I am informed by a well-placed source who has chosen to remain anonymous that there is hardly a woman who doesn't long for dalliance, languid caressing, and ballroom dancing. You will hardly ever go wrong in loving a woman, or other sentient creature, if you take your time and pay exquisite attention to every detail. (There is a reported move among feminists to make the country-western song "I Want a Man with Slow Hands" the national anthem.)

As women increasingly become captive to the staccato rhythms of the machine-driven market economy, they become as speedy as men—hard, driven, fast to come and go—and grab a "zipless fuck," as Erica Jong named it. As Leadbelly sang, "Those high-powered women sure got to borrow love and go."

Sadly, both genders are becoming increasingly "liberated" from leisure and freed from the duty of fondling their children, taking long vacations, sitting quietly and thinking about nothing practical, trembling at the thought of death, and spending entire afternoons making love. The habits and dispositions that spell success and self-esteem for the modern up-and-coming (or -going) person depend on keeping the throttle at full speed ahead. The type A personality that is aggressively involved in an incessant struggle to achieve more and more in less and less time is marked by a habitual sense of urgency, numbers, speed, and dead-lines and by less whole-hearted attention to anything.

Love ambles. Power runs. We invented speed in a futile effort to outrun death. When we make love of any kind, we enter a time-free zone, and death must wait outside and watch the clock.

In Hermann Hesse's novel *Siddhartha,* the young spiritual seeker Siddhartha spends years in dedication before deciding to take up the life of a householder. When he applies for his first job and is asked for his credentials, he replies, "I can wait; I can think; I can fast."

Pausing, waiting, and taking time *(kairos)* are necessary to develop the art of love. We cannot have carnal knowledge of each other without honoring the rhythms of our bodies. We cannot love "the environment" without paying attention to the habits of sparrows and spiders. Why should we expect love-making to require less silence and patience than waiting to catch a glimpse of a wild fox moving across an open field?

Men and women have made war on each other for so long that much of what is most precious now hides itself. Wild and tender things have retreated into the forest and will reveal themselves only to those who respect their shyness. Each of us lives within a private sanctuary into which we invite only those who pay full attention to us and who wait patiently until we open the door from the inside and welcome them.

ATTENTION AND HEALING

Listen once again to the common litany of childhood: "Momma, come see me dive into the water! Daddy, watch me run!" Before we learned to be ashamed of or to repress our desires out of fear of rejection, we unabashedly demanded the attention of adoring eyes. We knew that to be was to be seen. And oh, the infinite difference between being watched and being watched over, between the prying eyes in whose gaze we felt small and vulnerable and the kindly eyes in whose ambience we felt secure.

A mother writes me: "When my son was an infant, I found that doing other things while he was nursing—such as reading or watching television—nearly always led to a poor feeding or even vomiting. Only if I simply attended to him while he nursed did the nourishment stick."

We never outgrow the need to be seen, heard, and attended to. Ignored, we become anonymous—without a name. The drama of our lives is played out on an ever smaller stage before an absent audience, until we finally fall into isolation, loneliness, and dis-ease. Or else we act-out our disappointment and demand attention by behaving in violent or bizarre ways. The more lovelorn a culture becomes, the more it will replace heroism with infamy and honor with notoriety. Lacking a community in which we are attended to and nurtured, the best we can hope for is Andy Warhol's fifteen minutes of public attention—fame or infamy.

The gift of attention is an anodyne without which we cannot be healed. If we are lucky, graced, and persistent, we find hearth and health in the acceptance of friends and family. Sometimes it becomes necessary to hire a surrogate lover—a therapist who is trained to give us the attention we need to heal us of the wounds we received from being ignored, smothered, or attended to in demeaning ways.

⌘

The Practice of Attention

✧ The discipline of attention begins with meta-attention. Cultivate the habit of interrupting yourself to take note of what you habitually notice and what you ignore. Spy on your own consciousness. Meditate on how you *invest* your consciousness.

✧ Do you habitually lavish your attention on ideas? Things? Persons? Colleagues? Clients? Customers? Friends? A lover? Family? On your body, mind, spirit? The goings-on in your community? God? The enemy? Money? Sports?

✧ If you were to chart the changing foci of your attention during the course of a day, what would the graph look like?

And if, to paraphrase Jesus, "where your attention is, there will your heart be also," what would your pattern of attention say about you? What priority would love have in the hierarchy of your days? How would you like to change your investments of attention, time, concern?

✧ Think back to the first time you made contact with a person whom you have come to love. Remember the moment in detail, and reconstruct it as a film producer or novelist would. How was the scene lit? What caught your attention? What did you feel? Were you attracted or repulsed by your first impression? How close or distant were you from the center of the scene? What other persons were present? As you reconsider this first contact in light of what you have come to know and love about the person, were your first impressions accurate or inaccurate?

DESIRE:
Erotic Attraction

⌘

Three things are necessary for the salvation of man: to know what he ought to believe; to know what he ought to desire; and to know what he ought to do.

—THOMAS AQUINAS

What, now, is the Noble Truth of the Origin of Suffering? It is craving. . . . But where does this craving arise and take root? Wherever in the world there are delightful and pleasurable things, there this craving rises and takes root. Eye, ear, nose, tongue, body, and mind are delightful and pleasurable, there this craving arises and takes root.

—THE BUDDHA

Happiness lies not in satisfying all of our desires but in separating the chaff from the wheat, winnowing destructive from wholesome desires, and practicing voluntary simplicity.

SCENE: *Desire Said "Follow Me"*

It was not love at first sight. It was sooner than that. I felt the rising tide of desire before my inventory of her parts was completed and assembled into the portrait of a person.

I'm still not certain what it was about her that first aroused me. Something about the square cut of her shoulders and her proud carriage suggested a kind of womanly strength that was both strange and appealing. Her dark undulating hair and floor-length navy skirt spoke of the currents of a river that swirled around large rocks until they were polished smooth.

I was divorced and dissatisfied, so I suppose my sudden desire for an attractive woman needed no explanation. But it was a bit puzzling. She was not the type of woman that usually appealed to me. Her body, a moderately Rubenesque landscape of rolling hills, curve upon curve, suggested luxury and ease. I generally preferred lean, angular women with a slightly ascetic look. It was in her favor that she, like (need I say) my mother and other women in my life, was a brunette. Blondes have always struck me as pigmentally challenged.

Had I been of a mind to interrogate my desire rather than pursue it, I might have discovered quickly that much of what aroused and fanned the flame was an intuition that she was what I wasn't, and vice versa. It was obvious that where she was curved, I was straight, where she was spontaneous, I was full of plans, where she was water, I was rock. But I might have understood some of the hidden threads that drew me to her had I thought about the first words I said after we were introduced: "Before you got here, we were doing an exercise in the seminar in which I asked each person to imagine how they would look if they were of the opposite sex. You are it. I think I would look like you if I were a woman." (This was later to be considered the winner in a most-original-opening-line contest.)

I wanted her and she wanted me through years of turmoil

before it dawned on us that the delightful differences that fed our desire also hid painful polarities. The mutual attraction of thesis and antithesis led to warfare before the contradictions lay down together in sweet synthesis.

But that is getting far ahead of our story.

Desire as Human Nature

What the Greeks called *eros* is the attraction that draws us almost hypnotically toward any object we believe will complete us. Unfortunately, *erotic* has come to have an exclusively sexual connotation and has lost its original, more universal reference. Romantic and sexual desire always involves a strong erotic element, but so does our craving for beautiful merchandise.

Whether we lust after Paula or a Porsche, the insistent quality of our desire is rooted in our unconscious assumption that if we can only possess her or own it, we will be content. Her sweet flesh and its leather seats and fast ways (0 to 100 in six seconds) beckon us with the promise that our present dissatisfaction will be replaced by future pleasure. What is empty will be filled, what is lost will be found. The two halves of the coin, long severed, will be rejoined so that we may finally purchase happiness. Falling in love, I know that Paula is the missing piece of the puzzle of my life, that the Porsche is the nostrum for my ennui. In erotic attraction the desired person or object always seems to be shaped exactly to fit the hole in my soul. Insofar as we are speaking about the erotic element, it is therefore perfectly accurate to say that "I love my sweetheart and I love bittersweet chocolate."

Plato created a colorful myth to call attention to this hungry and urgent aspect of erotic love. Once upon a time, he said, human beings were joined back to back in three types of dyadic units—male-female, male-male, and female-female. These Siamese pairs were very powerful and could move swiftly by turning cartwheels on their four arms and four legs. But they were frustrated because they could never turn and face each other. Zeus took pity on them and sent a thunderbolt that split them into separate persons. Since that time we have been driven by a longing to find our missing half. Men seeking women were originally joined in a heterosexual dyad, while men seeking men and women seeking women were joined in homosexual dyads.

This myth of the androgyne is rooted in what premodern peoples considered obvious—we are *interdependent beings*. We are essentially incomplete, fragments of a whole. Eros is the motive-power that drives us in a restless search for the lovers, friends, and strangers who are the lost members of the community to which we belong. Our painful sense of separation from one another is a dis-ease from which we are healed by the great god Eros.

The unique quality of human *eros* shows us that we are metabiological animals. We continue to be racked by desire even when our basic biological needs have been satisfied, and thus we are perpetual exiles, incomplete creatures. The bottom line is that human desire is not psychological but ontological—rooted in our *being*. Therefore, insatiable.

AMBIGUITY: *Destructive and Wholesome Desire*

Romantics and shoppers in the Mall—the modern Temple of Desire—in quest of the perfect partner or the perfect wardrobe are prey to disappointment because no sooner do they possess the object of their affections than their desire returns and goes hunting for another object to excite it. As the Buddha said, "Desires are inexhaustible." When we satisfy one desire, another springs up to take its place, and another, and another, ad infinitum.

The excitement, the adrenaline rush, of erotic attraction rescues us for a time from confusion, boredom, or anxiety and sets us moving toward some new promised land. Like the rapids of the Colorado, desire sweeps us into a narrow canyon filled with beauty and danger. We can neither gauge its depth nor see where it is carrying us. Riding the crest of the wave may carry us to the calm water beyond the rapid, or shipwreck us in a whirlpool. To be safe, we need to know when to portage around a rapid, when to surrender to the current, when to paddle upstream, when to rest in an eddy.

Desire is a two-faced god, a heavenly and/or demonic power—a blessing or curse, an anodyne that may heal or sicken us, an impulse that may drive us in creative or destructive directions.

Anyone who has ever been in the grip of an addiction (and who hasn't?) knows how devious and destructive strong desire may be. The craving for a drink, a drug, sex, fame, or money may narrow our perspective and focus our energy on getting the "fix" we must have, even if it destroys both our own creative potential and the lives of those we love.

But desire may also lead us into the path of creative self-fulfillment and spiritual contentment.

When Joseph Campbell said, "Follow your bliss," he wasn't advocating hedonism or an obsessive pursuit of easy pleasure. He was, in fact, restating an ancient spiritual admonition that we should look to our deepest gifts and talents and follow our vocation—our calling to fulfill our most creative potential. The "holy spirit" is nothing less than the aspiration to become our best self. We would do well to redefine rather than abandon the old notions of sinner and saint. "Sin" is any inordinate desire, addiction, or obsession that sunders us from ourselves and others. A saint is a man or woman who is filled with wholesome desires, who is moved by *eros* to become capacious, creative, magnanimous, and fully alive.

Unfortunately, when we think about love we frequently use the model of sexual desire that tends to be intense and volatile. In fact, intense romantic or sexual desire may play only a minor part in the lifetime of any person devoted to becoming a lover. There are even modes of love, such as charity, that are primarily motivated by compassion and that contain very little erotic desire. We may care for the homeless and helpless not because we desire them but because they need us.

Desire comes in all degrees of intensity, from gentle to violent. The distance that separates liking from lusting, enjoying from grasping, or affection from addiction determines whether our desires lead us toward deep satisfaction or self-destruction.

Consider how steady, strong, and fulfilling is the desire that draws us to our friends. Friendship, or what the Greeks called *philia*, is made up of easy conversation and simple liking. In the presence of our friends, we put aside pretense and performance and become our best self. We laugh harder, create more easily, think better, and dare to feel the deepest sorrows and joys. Friendship is seeded in weeks, ripens in years, and grows stronger over decades. It knows none of the baying-at-the-moon madness, the possessiveness or jealousy that haunts romantic love. Step by step it opens a path that goes between our emotional depths and heights.

The desires that draw us to our friends, to teachers, to heroes and sheroes we admire, are a major source of the ideals that lead us to aspire to be our best self. Love can make us strive to be worthy.

Desire is very confusing because vital attractions and fatal attractions begin the same way, with our being drawn to someone or something we do not know. The benevolent bond that is forged between lovers and the malevolent bond that binds victim and victimizer both begin with a glance, an instant attraction, and the gift of attention. Strong erotic attraction to a person or object is a mystery waiting to be unraveled, an encrypted message about our incompleteness.

Strange to say, the roots of our most insistent desires are hidden from us. The reasons we are attracted by certain people and repulsed by others are complex.

For instance: Several years ago, Dr. Ofer Zur and I conducted a survey for *Psychology Today* to find out what qualities distinguish Excellent, Good, Average, and Inferior men. A majority of men and women who replied listed wisdom and compassion as the most desirable traits in a man. What surprised us was the number of letters we received from women who said, in essence, "I admire men who are honest, tender, and nurturing, but for some reason I don't understand, I am attracted to biker types, men who are rough and inconsiderate and macho. Why?"

The roots of our desires go so deep into our unconscious, into the substrata of our forgotten memories, that we may have no idea why we desire one person rather than another.

One day I was walking down Market Street in San Francisco when a fairly ordinary-looking middle-aged woman caught my eye. Unaccountably, I was strongly attracted to her, and as she passed me, I noticed a redolence of some perfume that opened a pathway through my limbic brain into some half-remembered time of heartfelt joy. As they say in the South, she "opened my nose," I fell instantly and eternally in love, turned around, and followed her. When I caught up with her a block later and we were waiting for the traffic light to change, I caught her eye and asked her, "Would you mind telling me what kind of perfume you are wearing?" "It is White Shoulders," she said. "Thank you," I replied. As she crossed the street and disappeared, I was flooded with memories. White Shoulders was the perfume my grandmother used to wear, and I was once again a small boy standing in back of Granny on the bed on the sleeping porch in Maryville, Tennessee, combing her long gray hair as she read to me.

What we identify as "love" is often a case of mistaken identity.

Many people wake up in middle age with the realization that in their youthful romances and early marriages, they were drawn to precisely the kinds of partners they were trying to avoid. All too often we marry stand-ins for our alcoholic fathers, shadowy replacements for our angry mothers, surrogates with whom we try to work out our unfinished childhood dramas. Or we fall in love with someone who incarnates the virtues and vices that are opposite our own. An orderly man who plans his days marries a spontaneous woman who lets things lie where they fall, lives in the moment, and is perpetually late for appointments.

INTERROGATING AND REPROGRAMMING DESIRE

Every wisdom tradition—philosophical, theological, or psychological—has as its heart the interrogation, clarification, and restructuring of desire. At the center of the Buddhist wheel of life, three figures represent the sources of alienation—a rooster symbolizes grasping desire, a snake symbolizes fearful aversion, and a pig symbolizes delusion. There can be no enlightenment without the practice of "right desire." In Christian theology Augustine sounded the warning against the spiritual sin of concupiscence—endless desire—and summed up the path to God by saying: "Love and do what you want." Freud founded modern psychology on the clinical investigation of the cacophony of desire produced by the clash between the unconscious and the conscious mind. He created psychoanalysis as a tool for forging a healthy harmony between competing desires.

Inevitably all of us need to reprogram some of our desires, to rewire our erotic circuits, to avoid what has habitually attracted us in the past and move toward someone or something we initially find unattractive.

SCENE. I first saw Betty at a picnic on the arm of a man I knew only slightly. Her tight velvet pants, low-cut blouse, swinging hips, and foxy mannerisms broadcast a seductive message, but somehow she did not strike me as sensuous or sexy. Several weeks later she came to talk with me about her relationships with men, and a sad story began to unfold. Her father had abandoned the family shortly after she was born, and she had seen him only two or three times, even though he lived in the same town. Her mother subsequently married four times and between marriages had live-in lovers, more than one of whom became sexually involved with Betty. When Betty left home at eighteen, she fell into the familiar but painful pattern of sexual relationships she had learned from her mother. With uncanny accuracy she chose men who initially seemed attentive and adoring but who became demanding, possessive, and abusive after a few months. The man with whom she was living was perversely candid about their relationship. "There is no way I am just going to be nice to her. She may not like it, but when I knock her around a little, it excites her and keeps her interested in me."

Betty's pilgrimage from destructive to wholehearted desire began when she entered therapy, began a period of celibacy, and took a long, hard look at her pattern of sexual involvement with men. In time she learned to ignore the aggressive men she was habitually drawn to and to pay attention to the kind of gentle men she had previously found uninteresting. Gradually the moth learned to seek the warmth of the flame without burning her wings.

THE PRACTICE OF WHOLESOME DESIRE

The move from destructive to wholesome desire involves developing several skills: (1) quiet observation; (2) distinguishing between what is merely habitual or addictive and what is satisfying and joy-giving; (3) reprogramming ourselves by cultivating wholesome pleasures.

✧ Take a long, quiet look at yourself and your relationships. Become the audience rather than the actor. Instead of being moved around like a puppet on a string by your desires, observe the drama of your love life from a great distance.

✧ What kinds of love relationships do you seek?

✧ Are you relatively content or filled with strivings?

✧ Which of your loves, enthusiasms, and passions are steady and wholesome?

✧ How much of your past and present belongs in the chapter of your autobiography entitled "Destructive Desires"?

✧ What addictions and irrational cravings (for alcohol, drugs, sex, gambling, money, fame, work, and the like) cause suffering for you and those you love?

✧ To reprogram your desires, experiment with different kinds of fasts and periods of abstinence. If it makes you anxious or depressed to contemplate giving up something other than the biological necessities—food, water, sleep, shelter—you are no longer free to choose between what is good, better, and best for you. Abstain from your habitual foods and fast for a day or two, and you will discover what you really want to eat. Practice celibacy for a while, and you may gain insight into how much your habitual mode of sexual expression contains a hidden agenda for possession, conquest, power, revenge, or security. Go into solitude and retreat from friends, family, and associates, and you will discover a lot about what kinds of relationships you really want.

KNOWLEDGE:
Mindful Love

In the mature account of love, it is only when one truly knows one's partner that love is given a chance to grow. And yet in the perverse reality of love (love that is born precisely before we know) increased knowledge may be as much a hurdle as an inducement—for it may bring Utopia into dangerous conflict with reality.

—ALAIN DE BOTTON, *ON LOVE*

SCENE: *Love Seeking Knowledge*

She—that female presence with the straight shoulders, proud carriage, flowing skirt, and long mane and legs, with hawklike but joyful face—she who had captured my attention, whom I had begun to desire, walked over, embraced Joseph, and began to talk to him.

I immediately began my investigation. Who is this person, this woman, whose shoulders speak to me of strength? What promise is suggested by her presence? I edged closer to eavesdrop and collect information. "I'm sorry to be late," she said. "The baby was sick, and I had to stay to take care of him."

"Damn it," I thought, "she's married. Bad luck." I moved nearer to Joseph, depending on his good manners to get an introduction. "Sam, this is my friend Jan Lovett. She has come up from Big Sur to take me to San Francisco after the seminar." "I'm glad to meet you," I said, "but I'm sorry to hear your baby is sick." "It's not my baby. It's a little boy I'm taking care of." "Oh," I said. At lunch we sat beside each other and began the choreographed dance of information exchange—light courtship. The quest, the questions began. Who are you? What brings you here? Where do you live? Why? Are you married? What work do you do?

Desire made me hungry for greater knowledge.

The Mindful Heart

Ancient philosophers argued a lot about the relationship between love and knowledge. The followers of Plato and Augustine maintained that we must love before we can know; the followers of Aristotle and Aquinas argued that knowledge precedes love. The issue can be convincingly argued either way.

In the Bible the word for sexual intercourse is the same as the word for knowing. Interpersonal knowledge is entering into the being of another. When I first met this woman, I did not yet know her enough to love her, or love her enough to know her. Ever so gradually over the next days, months, and years, desire and ignorance gave way to love and knowledge.

Love and knowledge are the interwoven threads of attraction and understanding that become the strings, the ropes, the hawsers that bind and bond us to each other.

Attraction is an invitation to greater knowledge. Love may be blind at first sight, but when it looks for a second time (respect), the mind begins to join the heart. A moment after she captured my attention, I began the quest for understanding.

Who is this fetching woman with the straight shoulders and the flowing ways?

Think of love as a fire whose intensity and ability to warm us is determined by the degrees of knowledge we add to the flame. The bits of information we gather in our initial contact are the sparks that ignite the tinder. To feed the fire, we quickly add kindling, the small sticks of data and facts about the person. Next, we collect more substantial branches—knowledge of the persona, the masks, the social roles, the presentations of self. Finally, if we intend to create a lasting friendship or an enduring marriage, we must bank the fire of desire with the dense oak of an in-depth knowledge of history and story.

Curiosity is foreplay. Love is not satisfied with superficial information or a casual touch of the flesh. It desires to enter the world of the beloved.

CULTIVATED IGNORANCE: *Idealization and Abstraction*

That love involves an endless quest for knowledge of the beloved is obvious if we look at its opposite, the ways in which we choose to cultivate ignorance—warfare, romance, and "sex."

War propaganda systematically eliminates the biography and the rich texture of individual human lives and reduces the other to "the enemy"—a demonic or faceless stereotype that can be eliminated without qualms.

Romance, which is the mirror image of reductive propaganda, elevates the other to an idealized image that we may prefer to the complex reality. In *On Love*, his classic philosophical analysis of romantic love, Stendhal describes a process he calls crystallization. A man, he says, will endow his lover

with a thousand perfections . . . regard her as something fallen from Heaven, unknown as yet. . . . At the salt mines of Salzburg, they throw a leafless wintry bough into one of the abandoned workings. Two or three months later they haul it out covered with a shining deposit of crystals. The smallest twig, no bigger than a tom-tit's claw, is studded with a galaxy of scintillating diamonds. The original branch is no longer recognizable. . . . Crystallization is a mental process which draws from everything that happens new proofs of the perfection of the loved one.

Stendhal goes on to discuss ways in which we cultivate blindness and denial for fear that accurate knowledge will shatter the illusion of perfection with which we have invested the beloved.

Not unlike romance, "sex" reduces the other to an abstraction, a body, that may be conquered and possessed or abandoned. The flood of popular and "scientific" literature about sex is filled with statistics that quantify the comings and goings of anonymous bodies and ignore the kaleidoscopic, intermingled meanings—the memories, dreams, disappointments, promises, hopes, shared stories—that distinguish human lovemaking from the breeding of domesticated animals.

In the continuing battle between the sexes, one of the greatest sources of alienation is men's and women's lack of knowledge about and empathy for each other. Gender propaganda abounds. Men and women stereotype, demean, and blame each other. Feminists and "liberated" men shout at each other with little will to understand. Strange as it seems, the majority of men are not curious about the inner experience of women. Few have listened to the cry and anger of those who have been judged "the second sex," the inferior gender, or savored the emerging spirit of creative feminism. Nor have many women considered the silent tragedy of the numbing of the spirit that afflicts men as a result of their unconscious acceptance of their assigned role as protectors and warriors.

THE UNITY OF KNOWING AND LOVING

Last night I awoke from a dream in which I had been pondering a fascinating and troubling question: What would it be like to be completely known and completely loved?

The theological imagination answers this question with a promise that we are loved by an all-knowing God. Ultimately, the only form of love that satisfies us is not blind but all-seeing: "His eye is on the sparrow, and I know He watches me."

Usually I find myself struggling to practice the kind of listening and information gathering that will allow me to move a small step inside the world of Jan or Jim. But there are moments when I catch a dazzling glimpse of the theological ideal of the unity of love and knowledge.

Circumstances threw me together on a regular basis with a man I found difficult to like. I was polite and even exercised my usual habit of trying to find out as much about him as possible. Still I felt no affection. One day, sensing my coolness, he confronted me and accused me of lacking compassion. "I don't think you have any idea of what it means to live for weeks on end in so much despair that you spend your time thinking how you can kill yourself," he said. "That is true. I don't," I replied. He then began to pour out story after story of his childhood, about how he had cringed in fear as he waited for his alcoholic father to return from work, about the beatings he had suffered and the continuous anxiety with which he still lived. By the time he had finished, my feeling toward him had changed. Knowledge had opened the door to compassion.

It is with some embarrassment that we must acknowledge

that we are as ambivalent about the possibility of being known as we are about entering into fully mindful relationships with others. Which one of us does not sequester a shadow of shame that makes us fear that "to know me is *not* to love me"? "If someone were to see me as I am," you may think, "with all my faults, brokenness, conceits, weaknesses, needs, feelings of worthlessness, and grandiosity, they would turn aside in disgust. Therefore I hide. Half of my life takes place in some closet or other, safe from the prying eyes of others."

The traditional gender ideals of the strong-silent man who plays his cards close to his chest and the mysterious woman who disguises her feelings with coyness go so far as to make a virtue of being unavailable and secretive. But wholehearted intimacy can develop only where two people are equally forthcoming and self-revelatory. To take the risk of loving, we must become vulnerable enough to test the radical proposition that knowledge of another and self-revelation will ultimately increase rather than decrease love. It is an awe-ful risk.

❧

The Practice of Knowledge

In its infancy love may be little more than a spontaneous feeling of liking and desire, an effortless attraction, an itch wanting to be scratched. But to survive and grow strong, it must be fed a steady diet of information and data. Love without knowledge is a sentiment without depth. To become a lover, you must become a private investigator and a connoisseur of life stories.

There are several experiments with the element of knowing that you might want to try.

✧ Pick someone with whom you have an intimate relationship but whom you would like to understand better. Pretend you are going to write the biography of, shall we say, your mother, wife, or woman friend. First, you will need to collect all kinds of historical information. (Where was she born? In what kind of family was she raised? What ethnic heritage? What were the pivotal events in her life? What was her relationship to her mother, father, siblings? What was it like to be a child who was abused–privileged, artistic–athletic, fat–skinny, pretty–ugly, blind–crippled, in a small town in North Dakota–in London, in—? Who were her friends? Lovers? Enemies? What were her struggles? Her wounds? Her humiliations? Her triumphs?) Once you have collected as much data as you can, begin to assemble her inner life story. How does she understand the drama of her own life? Does she tell her story as a tragedy, a romance, an irony, a comedy? Is she a victim of circumstances or an architect of her own destiny? And so on. Notice what happens to your own feelings as you gather more knowledge and begin to understand her life story. Does increasing your knowledge about her also increase your love?

✧ The next time you find yourself seated beside a stranger on a train or airplane or in some place you expect to be together for an hour or more, secretly gather as much information as you can about him or her. Imagine that you are a spy from the Commonwealth of Love, and your assignment is to learn as much as you can about the history, the present circumstances, the philosophy of life, and the values of your companion. Ask questions. Exercise your curiosity. Draw your companion out. Listen with your third ear to see if you can detect the script by which this person understands his or her life. After your companion departs, review what you have learned. How has the process of gathering information made you feel about your fleeting companion? Has what you learned made you want to know more? Has it made you feel affection or repulsion? Was there a brief moment of friendship? Every stranger is a world waiting to be explored, an invitation to a journey.

As you exercise your curiosity about people and become a connoisseur of life stories, you will develop a more interactive style of relationship.

✧ How open are you to being known? What secrets do you have? Who do you imagine would despise you if they knew the hidden truth about you? (You may be right!)

✧ Remembering that no less a lover than Jesus advised us not to throw our pearls before swine, and that self-revelation should be done with discretion, with whom would you like to take the risk of being more vulnerable?

Sensuality:
Being in Touch

I sing the body electric . . .
Head, neck, hair, ears, drop and tympan of the ears,
Eyes, eye-fringes, iris of the eye, eyebrows, and the waking or
  sleeping of the lids,
Mouth, tongue, lips, teeth, roof of the mouth, jaws and the jaw
  hinges,
Nose, nostrils of the nose, and the partition,
Cheeks, temples, forehead, chin, throat, back of the neck, neck-
  slue.

—Walt Whitman

Scene: *Making Sweet Sense of You*

I liked what I saw of her—straight shoulders, long hair, strong body, flowing movements. But the eyes control only twenty percent of the vote in the forum of the senses. As she greeted her friend Joseph, her voice rose to a pitch of enthusiasm punctuated by small squeals of delight, then fell into a tumbling cascade of words explaining why she was late. No monotone. The variation of pitch of her conversation was easy on the ear. Later, when I listened to her playing, the timbre of the flute was added to the repertoire of the sounds of her being. My ears voted yes.

Because I was raised in the South, where smell is recognized as an important sign of love, I have learned to pay close attention to olfactory testimony. If you do not like the smell of a person, you are unlikely to be comfortable in an intimate relationship. When I got within smelling distance of her, I detected a whisper of a perfume I did not recognize—a hint of grass on a windblown hill, with a whisper of gardenia, mixed with an equal part of sweat, sweet from excitement rather than sour from fear. Thank God, no deodorant or hair spray destroyed her natural aromascape. Much later, after I had become a connoisseur of her smells, I learned to make myself scarce when her breath and taste became metallic and to approach gently when her skin gave off a particular pink-purple glow, like the closing moments of a sunset, and her scent turned warm and pungent. All in all, my nose was opened, pleased with the fragrance of her being, and cast its ballot for a redolent relationship.

When we moved into the dimension of touch, I encountered my first ambivalence. My hands were accustomed to taut and sparse bodies like my own, and she was, on the surface, soft to the touch, the tough core of her resolve hidden beneath rounded flesh. Dancing with her was not easy. She moved to rounded Latin rhythms, I to the sleepy cadence of Dixieland. In time we grew familiar with the touch and rhythm of each other, and her permissive contours and my ascetic angles learned to play harmonious counterpoint.

By an overwhelming majority, the forum of the senses approved the candidate on the first vote.

RECLAIMING OUR SENSES

Those of us who are blessed and cursed to be "modern" men and women have been infected with an enormous confusion about love, sensuality, and sexuality. What we insist on calling progress has required people in the most "advanced" countries to weaken their connections with place, community, family, and friends in order to become workers and professionals who exchange their time for consumer goods and services. Increasingly we become a culture in which success depends on our willingness to become specialists who can function smoothly in abstract environments.

We dwell, ill at ease, within a haunting series of paradoxes.

• The more technological power we accumulate, the less our ability to control its social and environmental impact. Our obsession with power increases our impotence.

• The new information and communications technology exiles us, cuts us off from the intimate, sensate world our body inhabits. Those who live by the screen will die by the screen.

• The more we lose touch with the rich sensate environment, the symphony of sights, sounds, smells, tastes that surround us, the greater our obsession with "sex." We forget that we may be sensual without being sexual.

• The more we become obsessed with sex, the more all forms of touching become inappropriately sexualized and therefore taboo or suspect. In the present high-tech, low-touch, high-sex climate, we are increasingly phobic about touching. Colleagues don't. Women may touch other women if they are friends. "Real men" don't touch other men unless they are gay or engaged in those ritual forms of warfare we call sports. Adults who touch children not their own are suspected of sexual motives.

The only homeland to which we can return is the one from which we are exiled. To reinhabit the kingdom of love, we must reclaim our senses and, literally, get back in touch with what satisfies and delights us.

Remember the small child you once and always were and long to be again. Climb back into the encompassing arms of Mother, the lap of Father, as they were in the beginning, are now, and evermore shall be in the depths of your being (whether or not they were in the actual time of your childhood). Our first and final definition of love is inseparable from the touch and smell of the circle of people within which we felt safe and secure. In the womb love was a pair of hearts dancing as seamlessly as Fred Astaire and Ginger Rogers, until the cataclysmic moment of birth when motherandchild became mother and child, and two began the never-ending search to become one again.

Once born (ever after longing to be twice-born), love became warm satin, skin on skin, mouth on nipple, encompassing arms, cuddling, nuzzling, smucho-smacho kisses on the belly, horseplay, lying under the covers in the valley of paradise between Mother and Father.

It is a mistake to believe that we ever outgrow the primal need to touch and be touched, to inhale the fragrance and hear the sounds of intimacy. Metaphysicians may speculate that we are fallen angels, immortal souls, or spirits too pure to be contaminated by gross matter; AT&T may promise that we can "reach out and touch someone" from afar; but our abiding experience is that we are creatures of flesh and blood and folding bone, who are born and slain by time and comforted in our brief days by nothing so much as the texture of skin on skin. Because we are spirit incarnate, and not platonic archetypes or ghosts on a holiday on planet Earth, our manner of loving always involves the flesh and the senses. And in that measure love always partakes of something that is innocent, sensual, and childlike.

In a distant region of our ever-present past, we remain newborn children of omnipotent parents who could and should (but often fail to) encompass us in everlasting arms. So it is that the great explorers of spirit remind us that unless we recover the benediction of touch, we cannot enter the kingdom of love.

And what of the manchild or womanchild who was denied the birthright of encompassing arms? What if there is only a vacuum or a wound where there should have been the blessedness of mother-and-father love, frigidity where there should have been warmth, abuse where there should have been primal pleasure? Paradise denied.

I fear that the triumph of the therapeutic worldview has caused us to focus so exclusively on the slings and arrows of outrageous childhood and the drama of family life that we are apt to forget that we may also be wounded or redeemed by the carelessness or kindness of a community or by the ugliness or beauty of the environment within which we live. Gracefully, we may be mothered and fathered by friends, neighbors, children, and lovers to whom we have no biological kinship. A man who had an abusive or absent father may find the touch for which he always longed in embracing his son or daughter. Nor should we ever underestimate the healing that we receive when we are caressed by the early morning sun or delighted by the scent of lilacs. We live within a matrix that usually offers us far more of the anodyne of sensual delight than we accept.

You can never tell when you will receive the benediction of touch.

I was in a walled courtyard in the small village of Trakar in Bhutan with hundreds of villagers, watching the cycle of sacred dances that come each year at harvest. An old man sat beside me, dressed in a worn, hand-loomed robe that was redolent of the lingering scent of open fires and the sweat of the buckwheat harvest just finished. Our eyes explored each other, lingering over unfamiliar clothing, trying to decipher features and translate the rich network of facial lines. Our smiles broke out at the same moment, and we looked at each other and shook our heads in pleasure and approval. And then he reached over and took my hand.

Quietly, with infinite attention, he examined my palms, fingertips, nails. Holding our hands side by side, he pointed to the contrast between the color and texture of his skin and mine. For a long time he caressed my hand, looked at me, and shook his head with obvious satisfaction. I was moved nearly to tears and responded by examining and caressing his hand. His ancient skin was smooth, his fingers muscular and pulsing with warmth.

When a young woman from the village came by, he pulled her down beside us and started to explain something to her. In her schoolgirl English the woman told me: "He asks me to tell you that since you and he cannot speak together, touch is the only way he can become acquainted with you." To this day I remember those minutes as a rare interlude of primal love, pure touch.

Touch and Healing

Touch is a powerful element in healing, and a lover or a physician of the body and spirit has the obligation to use it wisely. Before religion became staid and medicine became "scientific," the "laying on of hands" was used both in ordination and in healing.

Several years ago I was invited to teach a course in medical ethics at the University of Florida Medical School in Gainesville. It soon became obvious to me that most dilemmas in medical ethics revolve around unstated assumptions about medical identity. What is a physician? What is illness, disease, cure, healing? In what ways do physicians sicken; in what ways do they heal?

In the seminar the question of appropriate medical touch emerged, and I devised a simple but radical experiment to clarify the issue. First, I asked each member of the class to examine the hand of another class member and give me an objective medical description of what he or she discovered. Second, I asked that they abandon the mode of objective observation and caress the same hand in a deliberately seductive and sexual manner. Third, I asked them to touch or massage the same hand in a sensual but nonsexual manner, intending to *give and receive* some measure of pleasure from the contact.

I then stated my hypothesis about the relationship between touch and healing. If you touch a man (or woman) only in an objective, scientific manner, you sicken him because you increase the alienation he already feels between himself and his body as a result of his illness. If you touch a woman (or man) in a sexual manner when it is inappropriate, you sicken her because you reduce her to a sexual object. The healing touch combines the quest for objective knowledge about the person with an intention *to give and receive* some measure of human warmth, reassurance, and sensual *(but not sexual)* pleasure. A physician may transcend the objective relationship between scientific expert and patient-as-body and establish a healing person-to-person relationship by the simple act of holding a hand while taking a medical history, giving a comforting touch to the skin after an injection, or stroking a forehead after administering a painful procedure. As embodied spirits, dis-eased by our illness, we need to remain in touch in order to be restored to health.

I was not surprised that my hypothesis about healing and

touch was considered radical by some of the medical students and obvious to others. It was debated for weeks. Cultures as well as individuals have different habits of proximity. In Italy it is customary for men to walk hand in hand or to embrace each other, whereas on Wall Street a handshake is as intimate as it gets. Americans, unless they live in California, seldom "press the flesh" when they have a conversation with a casual acquaintance and do not greet each other with a holy kiss, as was the habit among early Christians. As a rule, we do not touch across the lines of class or color, and we keep the maximum distance possible between ourselves and the homeless and the unfortunate. When a friend complains of a headache or sore arm, we do not lay hands on the offending flesh to knead, soothe, and comfort. When we fall sick, we are sent off to a hospital and wrapped in an antiseptic bubble, where we may be prodded, poked, and palpated but not caressed.

To reclaim the healing legacy of touch, we need to distinguish between sexual and sensual enjoyment and relearn the ancient sacred art of the laying on of hands.

SENSE AND SACRAMENT

We understand the depth of touch only when we combine the ideas of delight and sacrament. Human beings are creatures of skin and spirit. For reasons that are encoded into our DNA, we outgrew our fur, gave up the thick pelt that might have protected us from the elements, and went forth naked into life. In some prehistoric Eden we learned to clothe our vulnerability, but beneath the veneer of silk and denim, our primal nakedness remains and with it the hunger of the skin and the instinctive knowledge that we are safe in the world only so long as we touch and are touched.

The moment we deny our vulnerability, ignore our flesh, try to reduce ourselves to our social functions—as CEOs, doctors, lawyers, merchants, soldiers—we create a subhuman rather than a superhuman order of things. Having abstracted ourselves from the fullness of being incarnate spirits, we inevitably treat other people as things that can be manipulated and used to fulfill our designs. Witness the perennial practice of reducing our rivals to inhuman enemies who can be eliminated with a clear conscience.

Grace-ful touch is always consensual, equally willed, welcomed, and enjoyed by all who share it. Each of us knows instinctively, when we are touched, whether we are being handled and manipulated, used and dishonored, or caressed and cherished. An embrace or a hand on the shoulder may be desecration if we are touched against our will, as a sign of power, and reduced to a body. Or it may be sacramental, an outward and visible sign of an inward and invisible grace, when we experience our flesh and the flesh of another as inspirited matter and take delight in touch.

◆◆◆

THE PRACTICE OF SENSUALITY

Caring for others involves taking delight in their beauty, sharing pleasure in being in touch.

◆ Educate your senses in myriad ways of caring. Become an expert in tacit knowledge, hands-on intelligence. If you listen to your heart and the wisdom of your body, you will know when compassion calls on you to wrap your arms around a grieving colleague or embrace a friend for pure joy.

✧ What is your sensuality quotient—SQ—and your style of touching? At what distance do you feel most comfortable with strangers, colleagues, friends, family, lovers?

Much of your sensual style and your tolerance for intimacy was formed early in life. Every family has its informal (usually unconscious) rules about touching, smelling, tasting, and how people should talk to each other. In some families meals were devoured with great gusto, sunsets were savored, and on Sunday mornings the children piled into the family bed and cuddled and played like a litter of newborn pups. In other families food was fuel, touch was taboo, and sensuality was forbidden.

✧ Return in your imagination to a time before you were ten years old, and re-create the tactile and sensual environment of your early childhood—the smells, sounds, colors, textures.

✧ What were the aromas of love? What did your father smell like? Your mother? What scents do you associate with care? Baking bread? Tobacco? Whiskey? Baby powder? Perfume? Freshly washed sheets?

✧ Who touched whom? In what ways? How much touching and cuddling was there? What did your mother's body feel like? Your father's? What physical punishment was there? Violence? Sexual abuse?

✧ How much permission did you get from your parents to be sensual as distinct from being sexual?

✧ What objects did you find beautiful? What textures delighted your skin? A teddy bear, a cuddle blanket, Mother's fur coat, denim jeans, a hot bath?

✧ Describe a friend, a lover or mate, and a child with whom you are now intimate, using only sensual language, without any evaluation. What aromas, tastes, sounds, and kinds of touch do you enjoy in your multiple modes of loving?

✧ How closely do you link sensuality and sexuality? Do you have permission to be sensual with members of the opposite sex without being sexual? With members of the same sex?

✧ Experiment with escalating the sensual element in your relationships. Without doing violence to your sense of proper proximity and boundaries, put your hand on a friend's shoulder, touch the arm of an acquaintance who is telling you a funny or sad story, hug your teen son (even if he is a hedgehog), massage the shoulders of someone who complains of a headache, walk arm in arm with your best friend. Open your nose and break the taboo against smelling. Become a connoisseur of human aromas. Listen to the changing tones, cadences, and moods in the voices of the people you meet during the day.

The world makes sense only when the senses make love.

EMPATHY:
The Loving Imagination

❧

The failure to register another's feelings is a major deficit in emotional intelligence, and a tragic failing in what it means to be human. For all rapport, the root of caring, stems from emotional attunement, from the capacity for empathy.
—DANIEL GOLEMAN, *EMOTIONAL INTELLIGENCE*

SCENE: *Imagine That I Am You, and . . .*

Desire drew us together, and it was not long before we were keeping steady company. Our early months were full of love-making and storytelling, touching and exploring each other's personal history. The more I learned about her, the more familiar and strange she seemed. We dovetailed. I lived in the lyrics of the song, she in the melody. I led with my mind, turned inward to spelunk in the caves of philosophy. She led with her senses, feeling her way through the confusion of her days. We blended together easily.

We also struggled fiercely. Small differences of opinion escalated rapidly into major conflicts. Once, on a camping trip, I built a fire near a dead tree. She said it was dangerous and should be extinguished. I assured her that I had made hundreds of fires in my many years of camping and that the fire was safe. She disagreed and accused me of refusing to listen to her. Once more I explained that in matters of fire-building I was an expert; I *had* listened to her; I disagreed with her opinion. She insisted. I yelled. She withdrew into stony silence. For days I tried to get her to talk about what had happened, but she would not.

When the distance between us became polar and we seemed to reach a point of no return, I examined my part in the conflict. I had acted arrogantly in the way in which I had insisted on my superior knowledge of fire-making, and I had hurt her feelings by not taking her suggestion more seriously. Once the battle was engaged, I had raised my voice to an insulting level.

I tried to jump out of my own skin to inhabit her world. Why had she retreated into silence? Why was she reluctant to talk about feelings, mine and hers? Why was it so difficult for her to admit that she shared the responsibility for the conflict?

I put pieces of the puzzle of her history together, then walked into the picture that emerged. I felt my way awkwardly into what I knew about the dynamics of her early life—her father's desertion before she was born, her mother's hurt and anger, her grandparents' care, and so forth. I tried to imagine the exhilaration of the Eastman flute student, the grim sadness of the nineteen-year-old at the death of her mother, the liberation of the flight attendant who left Cincinnati to walk on the wild side of Miami and Esalen. And above all I tried to imagine how she experienced herself, what part she played in the drama of her own life.

SCENE: *A Taste of Yak-Butter Tea*

Hiking high in the Himalayas, I come across a group of large black woolen tents that house the families of yak herders who have brought their animals up into the lush pastures for the summer. A man, a woman, and two small children dressed in smoke-blackened clothes gesture to me, inviting me into their tent for buttered tea and conversation. We sit around an open fire. They bring out their best cup and wipe it clean with a dirty towel and hand it to me. First, they pour a finger of strong aniselike liquor. I drink. Three times the ritual is repeated. Then come tea and roasted millet. With gestures and pantomime I find that the man shares his wife with his three brothers. The radiant faces of the family bespeak a joy in living that I find rare in my world. Inhaling the smoke, taking the smell of earth and bundled bodies deep into myself, I begin to wonder and imagine what it would be like to live this way.

The Imaginary Journey into Thou

Empathy is that capacity of the *imagination* that allows us to share the experience of someone we love or someone with whom we may have no sympathy.

It is possible to know a lot *about* someone whom we understand very little and appreciate even less. These days any sophisticated computer expert could gather all of the data and facts that make up my curriculum vitae—family history, job record, romantic history, test scores, psychological profile, financial records, purchasing habits, and so on. But this collection of superficial knowledge would not necessarily yield any deep understanding of who I am as a unique human being.

Before we can love in any way other than the dependent way in which a child loves a parent, we must move beyond knowledge *about* to an appreciation *of* another person's life experience.

Empathy is the first of the skills that a therapist, a novelist, or a lover uses to get inside the skin of another person. Using all of the knowledge we manage to gather—hard facts, stories, images, impressions—we must then project our self into the inner life of the person we are seeking to understand and/or love. To practice empathy, we need to assume that every life story makes some kind of sense from the perspective of the person living it, and go in quest of the hidden coherence. How does this person experience herself and her world? What is her inner story, her personal myth, her self-image, her philosophy of life, her worldview, her value system? What makes her tick?

The role that empathy plays in our coming to know and love others parallels the role that fantasy has in our coming to know and love ourselves. To explore the multiple possibilities and unknown potentialities of my life, I must allow my fantasies and dreams free play. Fantasy, the Walter Mitty of the personality, allows me to sample many lifestyles and values without having to commit myself to any. To explore other people with whom I might develop mutual love, I must allow my empathic imagination free play.

COOL-HEARTED EMPATHY: *Love at a Safe Distance*

Empathy is one of the most overlooked and misunderstood elements of love and is often confused with its cousins—sympathy and compassion. But where sympathy is a warm feeling of a shared vibrational frequency, and compassion is an ardent feeling of solidarity in suffering, empathy is deliberately cool.

One of the more difficult challenges to my capacity for empathy came when I was working on the PBS documentary *Faces of the Enemy,* in which we were exploring how viewing other people abstractly as "the enemy" contributes to crime and warfare. One morning I picked up a newspaper and found the perfect horrible example for which I had been searching. A young man who had been heavily influenced by the rabid anti-

Communist propaganda of the radical "Christian Patriot" movement had entered the house of a prominent lawyer whom he considered (wrongly) to be a Communist and a Jew and brutally murdered the man, his wife, and their two children.

I contacted the young man's lawyer, the prosecutor, and other authorities and, after waiting four months, received permission to interview him in prison prior to his trial. Several days before the interview was to take place, I discovered that I had a passing acquaintance with the brother of the man he had killed. So I entered the jail with trepidation, resolved to remain professionally detached. During the interview I questioned the murderer about his association with right-wing hate groups and the propaganda that had led him to undertake his self-appointed "military" mission against "the Communists." I came away with a sense of the terrible logic of the paranoid mind, and I was chilled by the man's numbness to the horror of his crime.

A month later the lawyers for the defense subpoenaed me and the film of the interview. They thought they could convince the jury that the man was so deranged, he did not consider that he was killing people, only ridding the world of Communists. The day before I was to testify, I demanded to be allowed a second interview and was given access to the police records and the psychiatrist's reports. As I read about the murderer's alcoholic parents, beatings, family fights, abandonment, isolation, futile efforts to find work, aimless wanderings, marginal romance with an anti-Semitic woman, and involvement with the Christian Patriots, I began to journey into the interior of his world. I tried to imagine what it would be like to live within the brutal environment of his childhood and the barren but enemy-infested landscape of his adult life. Gradually I began to understand how and why his paranoid world made sense to him. For a time, by suspending my own values, feelings, and beliefs, I was able to get a glimpse inside his tragically twisted mind. But as my empathic understanding gave way to compassion, I became caught in a tragic dilemma. I was convinced that the man was guilty of a horrible crime for which he must be punished, yet I felt a terrible compassion for both the victims and the perpetrator, for the innocent and the guilty alike.

There is no guarantee that empathy will lead us in the direction of sympathy, compassion, respect, and care. Having violent offenders listen to the heart-wrenching accounts of the victims of their crimes sometimes elicits sympathy from them. But empathy may as easily lead to antipathy and help us make war rather than make love. Empathy, like paying attention, curiosity, and gathering data, is merely a prelude to love. It is, as philosophers are fond of saying, a necessary but not a sufficient condition.

It is precisely the cool, detached, voyeuristic quality of empathy that makes it a crucial skill in the art of loving. Empathy allows us to take an imaginative journey abroad while remaining emotionally secure at home. Our tentative forays into the lives of others let us sample relationships, play with possibilities, and anticipate problems before we ask our will to commit to something with serious consequences. This journey may serve to inoculate us against romantic illusions, to look before we leap, to steer our hearts in wise and hopeful directions. Only a fool gives his heart indiscriminately to every passerby.

Good detectives and generals, no less than lovers, must be experts in the practice of empathy. General Ulysses S. Grant said, "I know Lee as well as he knows himself. I know all his strong points and all his weak ones." The great tank battles of the Second World War were fought inside the minds of General Patton and General Rommel as they tried to understand each other as much as in the sands of North Africa. By contrast, in his memoir *In Retrospect,* former Secretary of Defense Robert McNamara reveals the complete failure of "the best and the brightest" to imagine both the mindset of the Chinese leaders and the Vietnamese longing for a free and unified homeland.

BECOMING SOMEONE ELSE

Novelists, actors, and therapists who use psychodrama can teach us a lot about how to develop empathy. The key to constructing a believable character in a novel or a play is paying intricate attention to detail. An actress must know the habits and the personality of the character she is inhabiting. How does she walk, talk, smile, frown? Does she drink coffee or tea or dry martinis? What were the pivotal events that shaped her life? What are her hopes, fears, and disappointments? Once the actress has this information, she creates the role by thinking, feeling, and imagining herself into the character. Use the knowledge you collect to *become* the person with whom you want to be empathic. Pay attention to nonverbal communication. Imitate posture, tone of voice, gestures, facial mannerisms, gait. You will find that pretending to be a character will gradually give way to a feeling that you *are* the character.

Consider a standard fight scenario that is as old as Cain and Abel. What Bob and Jane are fighting about doesn't matter. Maybe Bob danced too close with another woman at a party or spent more than they could afford on a new suit. Harsh words give way to loud voices. Jane criticizes him and demands to know why he did it. He retreats, becomes silent, walks away, and refuses to talk about it. She seethes and becomes icy. Since, with minor variations, this same scene has been repeated a hundred times in the ten years they have been married, we may assume that nothing is going to change so long as both parties to the conflict maintain their points of view.

The only hope is a new approach. Jane decides to try to understand why Bob withdraws at the first sign of conflict and refuses to deal with the issue. Why is he so terrified of the slightest display of criticism or anger from a woman? She reviews all the stories he has told her about his childhood. Gradually she homes in on one of the many scenes he has described, in which his mother in a drunken rage screamed at him and slapped him. He ran away, hid under his bed, and waited for the storm to pass.

Jane imagines the scene in detail, then begins to reconstruct the mind and stance of the frustrated mother, who feels caught in an unhappy marriage and is trying to drown her pain and loneliness in alcohol, and the world of the little boy. She then begins to reenact the scene, acting and speaking the parts of both mother and son.

First Jane assumes Bobby's stance and perspective. Sitting on the floor, she imagines she is playing with a toy car and glancing up at Mother, hoping for some sign of affection. "What are you making, Mommy?"

"What's it look like I'm making? Dinner. Just like I always do, every night of the year. . . . Goddamn it, Bobby, I told you a thousand times not to play in the kitchen when I'm trying to make dinner. Don't you ever listen to me? What's the matter with you? You're just like your dad."

Bobby (played by Jane) winces at his mother's words and gets up to leave the room. As he edges around the counter to stay out of striking range of his mother, he knocks over a mixing bowl full of batter.

"Oh, shit. Now you've done it!" she yells, slapping Bobby as he runs from the room. "Get out of my sight, and don't come back!"

Bobby (played by Jane) runs upstairs to his room, locks the door, and crawls under the bed. At first he cries softly, but then he curls up in a ball and lies still.

By placing herself within this scene—imagining the dialogue, the postures, the emotions of Bobby and his mother—

Jane begins to understand why Bob is so terrified of criticism and why he seems to freeze whenever she confronts him. As her new-found empathy gives rise to compassion for the hurt boy who still hides within the man, Jane is able to change the way in which she approaches conflicts in her marriage. Instead of criticizing and blaming Bob when conflicts arise, she shares her feelings of hurt and disappointment and her desire to be close. When Bob no longer feels that he is under attack, he is empowered to remain present and deal with the real issues that are fueling the conflict. Of such honest wrestling with problems, strong bonds of love are forged.

Practicing empathy requires an interesting combination of self-awareness and self-forgetting. The sensitivity of an instrument determines what it can measure. We can understand, tolerate, or forgive in others only what we have in some measure recognized and accepted in ourselves. The greater our emotional depth, the greater our capacity for empathy. There is also a need to bracket our ego, our values and views, and allow ourselves to "become" the other, to let go of our independent judgments and worldviews and identify ourselves with the other person's point of view. A great actor or mime must put self aside, become plastic, and conform body-mind-emotion to inhabit the character.

It is rumored that empathy is one of the great aphrodisiacs. A friend of mine who is reputed to be beloved of women told me that it often takes him all day to prepare to make love. "I begin early in the morning reviewing everything I know about my lover's life, her childhood, her struggles, her disappointments, her wounds, her triumphs, her hopes. As I go through this process, I realize how she has lived with integrity, and I am filled with respect and admiration. Once this feeling is present, I begin to make casual contact with her. I stroke her neck or touch her thigh or kiss her lingeringly. Each time I make physical contact, I see in my mind's eye the sorrow and the joy of her life. By nighttime, I feel privileged to be with such a person. And then there are no barriers or inhibitions. My technique is to appreciate her essence, to love her completely. No one can resist being known and loved fully."

❧

THE PRACTICE OF EMPATHY

There are endless occasions for practicing empathy.

✧ Think of empathy as a first step in practicing the golden rule that is central to every world religion. To "love your neighbor as yourself," make an effort to understand your neighbor's worldview and self-image and respect it as much as your own.

✧ Empathy, like charity, should begin at home. Start with a troublesome conflict you are having with your mate, your parents, or your child that never seems to be resolved. Instead of either defending your own position or criticizing, attacking, or blaming your "loved" one, switch sides and become the advocate for your intimate-adversary.

✧ Place yourself within the life story and emotional ambience of your father, who was cold and emotionally distant from the family. Imagine this is your story: "I was only eighteen and had been married for two months when I was drafted, sent to boot camp, and shipped off to the South Pacific. During the next two years I was in three invasions, including Guadalcanal, where we lost sixty-three men in my outfit and fought for weeks without relief. I was on Tarawa when I got the letter telling me that I had become a father. I guess I was happy, but it all seemed so far away. When I finally got home after the war was over, I was a different person from the boy who had left. There was no way I could explain to my wife or friends what I had been through—the horror of living in the middle of the killing and the dying. So I didn't talk about it. I settled in, got a job, and lived alongside a wife who was a stranger and a son I never got to know."

✧ Your teenage daughter wants to stay out all night at a beach party with her friends. Your immediate adult reaction is to say no. Before you do, pause, and imagine yourself back into the adolescent mind.

✧ Use empathy as an aphrodisiac. Put aside thoughts about the kinds of sexual behavior that excite you, and imagine switching bodies, emotions, values, erotic tastes, and world-views with your lover.

✧ Try to break free of the numbed detachment with which you habitually watch the morning news, and adopt a stance of empathic participation. Inhabit the central character in the story of the day: the wife who kills her abusive husband, the gang member who does a drive-by shooting, the eight-year-old girl who refuses to speak after being rescued from a bombed building in which her family was killed, a brother and sister who were separated as children when they were put in a Nazi concentration camp and are now reunited after fifty years. Live vicariously.

✧ On any rainy day when you are in need of the equivalent of an aerobic workout for your imagination, plunge into a great novel. Get inside the mind and heart of some of your favorite literary characters—the brothers Karamazov, Lady Chatterley's gamekeeper, Robinson Crusoe, John Grady Cole. . . . Remember, you do not need to approve of the values or actions of a person in order to inhabit them vicariously, any more than actors or novelists need to condone the actions of the characters they create.

Compassion:
Sympathetic Suffering

All beings tremble before violence. All fear death. All love life.
See yourself in others. Then whom can you hurt? What harm can
you do? He who seeks happiness by hurting those who seek happiness will never find happiness. For your brother is like you. He
wants to be happy. Never harm him, and when you leave this
life, you too will find happiness.

—The Buddha, *The Dhammapada*

Time like a rolling stream
Bears all its sons away.
They fly forgotten as a dream
Dies at the opening day.
—Isaac Watts, *Psalm 90*

Scene: *Love Among the Mortals*

Full moon in autumn, the aspens turning gold, winter nipping
at the edges of the night.

Two-thirty A.M. From fathoms deep in sleep, I hear the pierc-
ing sound of the telephone and struggle to the surface of consciousness, breathless with panic. Who is calling at this

ungodly hour? The faces of everyone I love flash before me. I remember the phone call that came in the autumn of 1964— "Your father is dying, come as quickly as you can."

It is bad news this time too: "Sam. This is Punky. There has been an accident. John Demetri got killed, and we're trying to locate his parents. We thought Gif might have his address. Is he there?"

"What happened?"

"He left here about an hour ago on his motorcycle and ran off the road down by Black Canyon. He hit his head on a rock. I tried to get him to wear a helmet, but he wouldn't do it."

"I heard Gif's truck come in a while ago, so I know he's up at his cabin, but he wouldn't have the address there. Why don't we wait until morning, and we will go over to John's house and see if we can find an old letter or something with an address on it."

"Okay, I guess that makes sense. There's nothing anybody can do now."

I hang up the phone and climb back into bed. The moon disappears behind the hill, and darkness deepens. I try to sleep, but waves of feelings and memories smash against my unbelieving mind, undercutting my illusions of safety, sweeping the ground from beneath me. Impossible! Not true! Just this afternoon John was painting my house. At five o'clock he was standing on the porch wiping the paint from his hands. The red-and-white cap he always wore that advertised Reed's Electrical Appliances contained a visible résumé of his recent odd jobs—a grease spot from the old Pontiac he was always working on, a sprinkling of sawdust from the cabinet he helped Gif build, brown paint from my house. His tattered Levi cutoffs matched his stringy beard and long stringy hair. Disheveled. A little like a lost dog who hadn't been well treated even before he left home. Gif always warned me: "You have to look underneath his appearance. John is a funny sort of guy. He always shows people his worst side first. He acts real stoned and stupid, but if you keep coming after him, you see he is a real sensitive man who has a lot of pain he is afraid to let people see." Several times while he was painting, John and I had talked about his dream of buying a few acres of land. I noticed that he looked pale even though he had been working all day in the sun.

As I review my sparse memories of John, sadness grows within me for the death of a man, for the shattered frail hope that had just begun to grow. And tears, because in the morning I must tell my son that his friend is dead.

At first light I give up the effort to sleep and get up to watch the sunrise. A tangerine glow from behind the mountain heralds the day. The stage lights change rapidly, bathing the valley in chrome yellow, chartreuse, lemon, topaz, daffodil, apricot, copper. With a hush, preceded by a hint of violet, the bronze and burning sun steps over the ridge and takes command of a day that is already haunted by absence. I drink cups of steaming tea and watch the drama from the privileged seat among the living, feeling unaccountably guilty and embarrassed by beauty.

As I walk up the path through the meadow to Gif's cabin, my mind squirms looking for the right words. How do I introduce my son to death? This man-boy, twenty-two years old, sleeps hard, dreams vividly, and wakes slowly. He doesn't like me to talk to him before breakfast. Should I break the news gradually? Give him time to come fully awake? Fortunately his dog, Rastas, sees me coming, barks, and warns Gif that their territory is being invaded. When I get inside the cabin, he is half awake.

"Good morning, son," I say, walking over to the bed and pausing until I can put my hand on his uncovered and vulnerable shoulder. "I have some real bad news. John was killed last night."

Gif looks at me in stunned silence. "On his motorcycle?"

"Yes. How did you know?"

"I was at Punky's last night playing pool, and there was lots of free beer. I knew John was going to Omak on the motorcycle to spend the night with a friend, so he could see about his unemployment checks in the morning. I tried to convince him to come home and drive up with me today, but he wouldn't do it. . . . Dead? He's dead?"

"Yes, son. It's impossible to believe, isn't it?"

"Yes and no. Somehow I'm not really surprised. He always said he would die young and violently. It was almost as if he knew. When he came into the bar last night, he took out a quarter and held it up and said: 'This is all the money I got, but I guess it's all I need since the beer is free and the loser is going to have to pay for the next game of pool.' I grinned at him, and when I started to leave, he said: 'What's the matter, Gif, you afraid to play me?' We traded friendly insults and played a game or two, and when I went out the door, he flashed me a big smile and gave me a thumbs-up sign. It was always like that. We understood each other, like brothers, without having to talk about it. Ever since he came back from Vietnam, he was in such pain that he stayed drunk or stoned a lot of the time. Once I told him: 'John, I can see all the pain and rage you have bottled up inside you.' And he said: 'I'm glad you can,' but we didn't have to talk about it after that. We were just friends. I think, somehow, it was his time to die. At least he's not in pain now."

Silence, again.

Gradually the awful fact begins to sink into Gif's heart, and he starts to cry softly. I also. I want to cradle him in my arms and protect him as I did when he was a baby. As I reach over and embrace him, I feel my body (calloused by frequent grief, covered with scar tissue from the death of my father and friends) form around his sinewy frame as if to shield him from tragedy. I hold him for a few minutes. But we are both too awkward to take comfort for long within each other's arms. We edge apart, trying not to notice each other's tears.

"It's a hard one, son. And when you get older, you still can't believe it, but you learn to expect it."

"I guess you never get used to death, do you, Dad?"

"I never have."

I sense Gif wants to be alone, so I leave the cabin. An hour later he comes down to the house, and I cook thick slices of home-cured ham and eggs and strong coffee. After breakfast we go across the county road to John's house to look for his parents' address, which we finally find in a stack of letters in the bedroom. As we turn to leave, I see that Gif has picked up John's Reed's Electrical Appliances cap and put it on his head.

The flood of sorrow carries us into each other's arms, and I hear a silent scream welling up from my depths: "Death, keep your goddamned hands off my son! You can have me, but leave my children alone."

Scenes from three generations of my history flash before my eyes. First, I see myself standing at my father's grave by a juniper tree in Prescott, Arizona, wearing his hat and cursing death. Next, I imagine myself as an old man standing on the high ridge above this farm, watching my children and grandchildren eating from the apricot and walnut trees I have planted, harvesting the memories of my care. Finally, I see myself turning and walking over to the pine tree under which I want to be buried and giving myself peacefully to death.

As my vision fades, I remember a Buddhist parable. A man comes to the Buddha and asks for a definition of happiness. The Buddha replies: "Grandfather dies, father dies, son dies." "That sounds like terrible unhappiness," the man replies. "No," the Buddha says, "this is the natural course of things, and that is the most happiness we can expect. Think of the sorrow if the son dies before the father, and the father before the grandfather."

Gif and I pat each other on the back to signal that it's time to move apart. Our embrace loosens. Seeing John's hat on Gif's head, I remember that the universe does not guarantee us a timely death and that our contract with life always includes the possibility of tragedy. And for the first time, I see on my son's face the marks of one who has been initiated into the knowledge of mortality. From this day forward, we will be bound together by the terrible and compassionate knowledge that we share the fragile gift of life for only a fleeting season.

SOLIDARITY IN SUFFERING: *Fellow-Feeling*

Compassion is born in the moment we recognize that all sentient beings suffer the dis-ease of mortality.

In our feel-good culture, emphasizing the link between love and suffering may seem morbid. Why not accentuate the positive, look for the silver lining, and visualize peace, prosperity, and pleasure for all? With a little Prozac if necessary. We would like to avoid suffering *at all costs,* especially in matters of love. But the price tag for ignoring suffering is life within a cocoon of sentimentality and illusion.

The young Siddhartha lived in the wealthiest section of town, not far from the Great Mall of America. As the only son of a two-career, multimillionaire, bicoastal couple, he enjoyed every luxury money could buy—good schools, fast cars, beautiful companions, designer labels, vacations in Disneyland, skiing in Aspen, unlimited credit cards, socially acceptable drugs. He was well on the way to living happily ever after, when he took a wrong turn that led him deep into the blighted, *Blade Runner*–like center of the city. His automobile suddenly stopped, leaving him smack in the middle of the human condition. Shaken. Disturbed. Unable to forget what he had seen. Restless. No longer satisfied with Everything. Lost.

The Buddha (né Prince Siddhartha), who was neither pessimistic nor joyless, proclaimed the bad news first: Existence is suffering. And the good news followed: There is a path that leads beyond (meaningless) suffering to wisdom and compassion, but you can't get there if you begin anyplace other than suffering.

Let's unpack this disconcerting idea to see if we can trust its promised balm.

Compassion begins with the acknowledgment of the single inescapable truth that is the foundation for the possibility of love between human beings—an awareness of the tragic sense of life. In that final surrender that marks the ego's defeat in the hard-fought battle to defend its illusions, we are forced to confront the implications of our mortality. Many small differences separate us one from another, but one large thing unites us. We are all citizens of the earth household, destined to dwell together in the democracy of death, in which there are no distinctions of race, color, creed, class, or gender. Without our consent we are formed by the iron laws of corrosive time, prey to decay and disease, and haunted during our brief days by the anxious knowledge that we are like the grass of the field. The syllogism—all men are mortal, Socrates is a man, therefore Socrates is mortal—places you and me in the same community as Socrates, my son Gifford, and his friend John.

Compassion is literally *feeling-with*, or being-with. We are first and foremost fellow-humans. *Mitsein*. Kinfolk. Kindred flesh. It is this radical fellow-feeling that creates the impulse that flowers into kindness.

Indeed, our compassion is not limited to our fellow-humans. Today I find myself uttering the Buddhist vow to be compassionate to all sentient beings. As I write these words, our year-old Jack Russell terrier sits in her bed beside me. Three days ago a rattlesnake bit her. Her head is still so swollen, she looks like a guinea pig. She sits in silent incomprehension, suffering from the effect of a cause she does not relate to playing with a snake. My heart goes out to her.

In the degree that we are moved by compassion, romantic love may be transformed into abiding care. Romance begins when we conspire to create an image of an ideal creature who is unmarked by ugliness, disease, time, or having to die. Being in love, we cultivate the illusion that by joining with the beloved we can "live happily ever after." In place of romance, compassion introduces us to the necessary suffering of love and therefore to abiding passion. To feel others' pleasure, I must be able to feel their pain. Only those who recognize each other as fellow-strangers-in-the-night can forge the bonds of true kinship and learn to be kind. And kindness, not wild abandon, is the essence of abiding passion.

COMPASSION FOR THE ENEMY

The flower of compassion can bloom at any moment, even in the ambience of enmity.

A friend told me a story of a kind that has been repeated countless times in the history of warfare. "We were in a firefight not too far from Da Nang. Charlie had us surrounded, and we were taking fire from every side. We called for air support, and the choppers came and rained death all over his parade. I got a clear shot at one gook and saw him fall. When everything was quiet, I went over to look at my kill. He was about twenty or twenty-five—it's hard to tell with slants—and he had on the black pajamas, so I knew he was pure enemy. But then I started going through his pockets, and I found a little packet of pictures, wrapped up in a silk handkerchief, of him and his wife and a couple of kids. After that it was a lot harder for me to go into combat. Sometimes, if I had to, I aimed for a leg or an arm, or if we weren't in danger, I just shot into the bushes. I've never been able to get that guy out of my mind. I can't get over the feeling that he was just like me. He didn't want to be in the goddamned war, and he didn't have anything against me except that I was in his country."

Compassion is apocalypse, the true revolution, the end of warfare and the politics of power. It destroys the hierarchy of values, the mythology of superiority, that is the basis for tribal and national society. It dissolves our political loyalties as citizens of (self-)righteous nations and gives us a new identity as members of a commonwealth of sentient beings. No more S&M, top and bottom, superior and inferior. The true revolution in human affairs can never come by armed violence because those who live by the sword will continue to live by the sword ad nauseam. The power game, in any of its forms, destroys the compassion that is the only basis for lasting community.

WISDOM AND COMPASSION: *Deconstructing the Ego*

Don't look for The Truth. That is too big an idea for human beings. Proceed as if you are rowing a boat. Let the truth remain behind your back. As you proceed forward, just keep pulling on the oars and pushing illusion away from you, and you will make gradual progress toward truth.

—GURU BAWA

The injunction to be compassionate seems to command us to do something that can only happen spontaneously. Isn't compassion a feeling, like joy or sorrow, over which I have no control?

The way out of this seeming dilemma lies in the link between wisdom and compassion. In Buddhist philosophy wisdom and compassion always appear in tandem because each is one side of a complex virtue. Wisdom, or enlightenment, is the shift in awareness that happens when I cease to hold to the illusion that I am a separate entity and recognize that I am an integral part of the web of being. Compassion is nothing more or less than the disposition and action that flow naturally from that perception. Since I exist only in relationship to other sentient beings, the essence of who I am is com-passion. My fellow-feeling is merely the emotional recognition of this fundamental fact of existence.

"Com-prehension" means grasping the pattern that connects. "Com-passion" means *feeling* the connections with one's fellow-beings. It begins to happen spontaneously when you give up the illusion that you are a solitary being and extend diplomatic recognition to all the members of the community of beings, without whom there could be nobody you call your self.

If you look carefully at the interrelations between your self and everything else that surrounds you, you will find that your ego, your sense of being a separate entity, begins to vanish as you realize that nothing exists except connections.

The old nursery rhyme, slightly amended, tells the story of co-being and co-dependence. This is the house that Jack built; this is the tree that grew the wood that went into the house that Jack built; this is the soil that held the roots of the tree that grew the wood that went into the house that Jack built; these are the worms that make fertile the soil that held the roots of the tree that grew the wood that went into the house that Jack built. This is the man that cut the tree that grew the wood that went into the house that Jack built; this is the saw used by the man who cut the tree that grew the wood that went into the house that Jack built; this is the refiner who produced the gas that powered the saw used by the man who cut the tree that grew the wood that went into the house that Jack built. . . . And so on, ad infinitum.

Meditate on your connection to and interdependence with

other people, places, and things, and you will soon discover that your "self" is more like a highly organized community of interconnected beings than anything that resembles a separate individual. Subtract symbiosis and linkage between you and other living entities, and there would be no you. As Alfred North Whitehead said, every "entity" is an "occasion." Individual beings are happenings within a larger happening we call a universe. We *are* the crossroads at which we meet. Subtract relationships, and you and everything else would vanish.

Wisdom and compassion emerge slowly as we dismantle or deconstruct our illusion of individualism, demythologize the worldview created by our false sense of superiority or inferiority, and disarm the fortress of the ego.

It was my discovery of Karen Horney's *Neurosis and Human Growth*, two decades ago, that gave me my first taste of the freedom that results from monitoring the crazy-making antics of neurosis (a modern synonym for *ego*). Horney taught me that neurosis always involves an oscillation between two opposite illusory senses of self, as superior and inferior, omnipotent and impotent, glorified and degraded, better and worse than others, stronger and weaker. I began to notice a cycle. One day I would be arrogant and judgmental and would consider myself superior; the next day I would feel shameful, small, powerless, and inferior. In comparing myself to others, I always judged myself as one-up or one-down. Never as equal. Other people were either my superiors or my inferiors. Not my fellow-beings. As I observed the ups and downs of my seesawing ego and studied the devices and defenses I used to elevate or deflate myself, I gradually learned to stand on the unmoving middle point of the fulcrum—to see myself as neither better nor worse but as one among many. Compassion is incompatible with comparison.

One barrier to compassion is the perverse comfort we feel in observing the suffering of others, based on our unconscious, infantile illusion that we have escaped because we are better than they. Watching the agony of Bosnia or the plight of the homeless, we secretly congratulate ourselves that our virtues have kept us from being cast among the unfortunates. We maintain a safe distance from anybody with bad luck, or bad karma, for fear of being contaminated. Look but don't touch.

But compassion destroys our safe observatory and submerges us in the community of the wounded and the mortal. It washes away the illusion that we are an island, and it situates us on the mainland. Do not ask for whom the bell tolls, it tolls for you—and me.

When we break down the walls, compassion flows of its own accord. The heart travels with its own passport, beyond frontiers, boundaries, checkpoints. It acknowledges no fatherland, no motherland. Not even time. We may feel compassion for someone long dead or little known. Most of us who are over forty can still remember the moral outrage and compassion evoked in us by the photographs from Vietnam of the young girl who had been napalmed running down the road, and the man about to be shot by the general.

❧

THE PRACTICE OF COMPASSION

✧ Observe the movements of your consciousness and moods as you go through the cycle of judging yourself alternately as superior and as inferior. How, when, and where do you play the superior one? The inferior one? What is the cost in your personal life of playing your particular version of the sadomasochistic game of top and bottom, one-up and one-down?

❖ What is the cost in political-economic-social terms of our refusal to create a politics of compassion? The psychological defense mechanisms and military budgets that defend us against "the others" squander the resources that could create a community of fellow-beings. Strange how we consider compassion politically impractical, when it is the only realistic basis for our survival.

❖ The great spiritual traditions speak with a single voice about the cultivation of compassion and urge us to meditate on death. Practice awareness of the impermanence of all things, and you will find that it becomes easier to break down the false distinctions, prejudices, ideologies, and tribal loyalties that separate us.

❖ Make a daily practice of remembering the suffering of others. Meditate on the men and women who at this instant are being tortured in prisons, killed in wars, dying of starvation, wandering homeless on the earth. Invite your far-flung kinfolk into the hospitality of your heartful imagination. Sit with them in their suffering and tragedy, and in time, you will discover something you can do to lessen the quantity of their pain.

ENJOYMENT:
Sympathetic Pleasure

Love to faults is always blind
Always is to joy inclined,
Lawless, winged and unconfined,
And breaks the chains from every mind.
　　　　　　　—WILLIAM BLAKE

SCENE: *The Biannual Meeting of the Mutual Enjoyment Society*

I met Earl on the wrestling mat at the Cambridge YMCA in 1957. From the beginning it was clear that we were going to have an odd match. At the opening bell he charged blindly, a 185-pound bull, took me down, and attacked from every angle in an effort to get a fast pin. All I could do was tangle my lanky 168-pound frame around him, keep low to the mat, and ride out the attack. When he began to huff and puff and the force of the onslaught diminished, I managed to escape and gain the upper position. Remembering the folk wisdom—"If you meet a bull, play him like a coyote"—I began to nip away at any leg or arm he left unprotected. Before long I got him in a punishing cross-face-arm-lock, drove against him, toppled one of his four supporting limbs, and began to muscle him over onto his back. But he didn't budge. I couldn't pin him, and he couldn't escape, so the match ended in a draw.

After the match we went out for a beer and discovered immediately that we were both graduate students at the Harvard Divinity School, he working on a degree in Old Testament studies and I on one in the philosophy of religion. Our conversation about theological matters rapidly became a mirror image of the loving combat we had engaged in on the wrestling mat. He had just arrived from Texas, full of the theology of Karl Barth and assured of the truth of the Bible and the Presbyterian Church. He wasn't hidebound, rigid, or pushy in his conservatism, but it never seemed to have occurred to him that the claims of Christianity should be seriously questioned. I was newly liberated from Calvinism, and my existential agony was near the surface. My doubts were running wild in every direction, generating irreverent and incessant questions. During several rounds of beer, we argued from opposite assumptions without coming to the slightest agreement, except that we would have lunch the next day and wrestle every Wednesday evening.

Come November, we added another activity to our weekly rituals of friendship. I was a veteran scuba diver, and Earl wanted to learn. So one cold Saturday we went out to a rocky beach on Marblehead, struggled into wetsuits, and plunged into the frigid Atlantic. As usual, Earl was enthusiastic. I say "as usual" because among his most engaging qualities were his insatiable curiosity and his talent for studying, trying, and appreciating new things. Like boats and diving. While I would ponder for a long time, Earl would just do it. Within a few weeks he had acquired a blunt-nosed aluminum boat that only a Texan would think was good for the New England coast, and we began to dive in rough waters on days so cold, we would have to sip brandy and hot tea when we came out of the water to stop shaking. We regularly caught our quota of lobsters and returned to a communion feast with our wives and families, during which the two of us frequently fell asleep from the exertion of the day, the shock of exposure to cold water, and a great plenty of wine and conversation.

After Harvard I went on to become a professor and later a freelance philosopher. Earl reincarnated every few years, in rapid succession becoming a seminary professor, chemical engineer, salesman, tutor, stockbroker, and finally amateur geologist—each time with gusto. Throughout four tempestuous decades—marriages, family crises, divorces, remarriages, career changes, a dozen moves—we have met to renew our friendship. In a couple of weeks I will be going out to Durango to ride horses and hike the mountains with Earl. He will initiate me into his latest enthusiasms—the joy of backpacking with goats—and he will instruct me in the flora, fauna, and rock formations of Colorado. I will bring the latest news from the explorers of the inner world. We will argue the virtues of different breeds of horses—Missouri fox-trotters versus Peruvian Paso Finos—and compare notes on marriages, children, and matters of the heart. We will pick up in midparagraph the threads of conversation we have been weaving for forty years. And sometime during our visit, we will, imperceptibly, step out of our normal reality, where we are haunted by a shadow of separation and loneliness, and enter a zone of contentment that radiates from the simple pleasure we take from each other's company.

Communion in Joy

Man was made for joy and woe,
And when this we rightly know
Through the world we safely go.
—William Blake

If, to develop compassion, we need to participate in the suffering of our fellow-beings, to develop sympathetic enjoyment we need to participate in the pleasure of others. If the first noble truth is *Existence is suffering*, the second noble truth is *Existence is en-joy-able*. Compassion is a reliable guide to life and love only when it is accompanied by its Siamese twin.

To catch that wily thing we call love, we need to weave a snare of words rich in contradictions and paradox. We need a complex warp of elements that are light and heavy, spontaneous and careful, gift and task, comfort and suffering. But the woof that completes the snare is composed of simple, strong threads—pleasure, liking, and enjoyment.

It is because friendship contains the largest quantity of enjoyment that it is the most stable and enduring of all the modes of love. As Robert Brain says in his classic treatment of *Friends and Lovers*, "Friendship, everywhere, makes the world go round—not love in its romantic, sexual sense. Romance so often seems to focus on lack, longing, and nothing so comfortable as enjoyment. As a woman friend said, 'Once, when I was entangled in a passionate and addictive love affair, my therapist kept asking, "But do you *enjoy* being with him"—which, of course was far from the case.' " Friendship demands no romantic frenzy, no howling at the moon. It depends on nothing so stout as obligation, as fragile as a pretty face, or as irrational as the thick sinews of blood and clan. It depends only on mutual delight.

RESENTMENT AND ANTIPATHY

At first glance it would seem that rejoicing with those who rejoice should be easy, while having compassion for the suffering of others is difficult. But strangely, we are often able to share the weeping and mourning of friends and strangers more readily than their laughter and dancing. Who has not been embarrassed to discover that he or she was jealous of the beauty, achievements, fame, wealth, health, or good fortune of a friend or even a lover or spouse? The unhappiness of others elicits our concern, but all too often we look on their happiness with green-eyed envy. It is as if we think there is a limited amount of good fortune for which we must compete.

Several years ago, through no fault of my own, my book *Fire in the Belly* spent some months on the *New York Times* bestseller list. The resulting touch of fame was an interesting and painful experience. My best friends celebrated the occasion with unambivalent joy. But many of my professional acquaintances were clearly envious and unhappy with my success. A high percentage of magazine and newspaper writers attacked the book without having read it. One day I expressed my puzzlement about the unearned resentment I was reaping to George Leonard, an old friend who had been an editor of several magazines. "It is a journalistic tactic," he explained. Many writers, driven by resentment, systematically put down anything that has become popular in order to make themselves and their readers feel superior.

In the degree that we compare ourselves to others and feel that we fall short in creativity, beauty, power, wealth, health, luck, fame, or intelligence, we are tempted to resent those who appear to have what we lack. Their happiness seems to be a judgment on our unhappiness; their richness makes us feel poor; their intelligence makes us feel dull. So rather than rejoicing in their good fortune, we criticize and cut them down to size in order to "get even." Resentment is the secret revenge we take on the happy when we feel unhappy, on the blessed when we feel cursed, on the powerful when we feel we are victims.

The problem is that it backfires. Some wag once defined resentment as "a poison we take in the hope that it will kill the other guy." Webster's definition shows us how the poison works. Resentment is "a feeling of indignant displeasure because of something regarded as a wrong, insult, or other injury." When we feel that our dignity has been offended by the pleasure another enjoys, we fill ourselves with displeasure, as if that would, by some kind of psychological black magic, cancel out the advantage the other person enjoys. In reality, all it does is push us further into our own suffering. Taking umbrage drives us deeper into the darkness of the wounded ego, which cannot be healed except by compassion and sympathetic enjoyment.

Resentment is antipathy, a kind of antifeeling or feeling-against that is the mirror image of the feeling-with that is the basis of compassion and sympathetic enjoyment. In love I am joined to another so profoundly that I can say, "Your suffering is my suffering, your joy is my joy." In resentment I am so alienated from another that in effect I say, "You deserve to suffer, and your happiness is stolen from me."

A thousand times we stand at the fork in the road and must choose the path of antipathy or sympathy.

SYMPATHETIC ENJOYMENT

We are reverberatory beings tuned to a common vibrational frequency or energy, much like the strings of a violin. Inevitably we amplify or diminish one another. Our word *encourage* encodes a vision of intersubjectivity in its suggestion that one person may hearten and give courage to another, just as *enjoy* bears testimony to the contagious nature of happiness. When we engage with others in a sympathetic way, we en-courage, en-hope, en-faith, em-power, and en-joy each other. When we engage in an antipathetic way, we dis-grace, dis-affect, dis-able, dis-ease, dis-compose, dis-orient, and dis-gust each other. For better or for worse, we are joined in a single body politic.

Between wholehearted lovers, pleasure is a Ping-Pong ball that gets batted back and forth. At its best, sexual love matures into generosity and sympathetic enjoyment. His enjoyment increases her enjoyment, which increases his enjoyment, which increases her enjoyment. At some point midway in the game, there is a quantum leap, and the actors disappear into the action; he and she become a unified nexus of mutual enjoyment, a reverberatory event. (You may adjust the pronouns to compensate for my heterosexual bias.) For two persons to enter into the reverberatory zone of sympathetic sexual enjoyment, they must share each other's joie de vivre, savor each other's stories, and honor the hopes that give each other a sense of meaning and worth.

Love gradually turns the heart into an echo chamber, in which the suffering and joy of two persons entwine to form a single systolic-diastolic rhythm.

At times, sympathetic enjoyment asks more of us than simply shared pleasure. Most often we share with those special people we enjoy a common enthusiasm for bowling or Bach. I enjoy being with a friend because I am entertained by his stimulating conversation and sharp wit. I enjoy a lover because of the pleasure she gives me. But in sympathetic enjoyment I travel beyond simple pleasure and enter into another person's self-understanding, self-valuing, and self-enjoyment. I vicariously share my friend's self-love. In some small measure I appreciate him in the same way and for the same qualities that he appreciates and enjoys his own existence. Finally, more than the pleasure of wrestling, riding horses, or conversing, it is the "Earlness" of Earl that I enjoy.

Wanting the best for a child, a friend, a mate, may bring us sadness as well as joy. As often as not, children must separate from their parents to seek their fortune elsewhere. It is with bittersweet emotion that I place my daughter, Lael, on the airplane that takes her back to Brazil, thankful that she has found her place but sad that it is in a country so distant. Even soul mates may come to a fork in the road where their paths diverge, and they must grant each other the hardest gift of fidelity—a loving divorce. In any long-term relationship there will be times in which the growth of one person will be disturbing to the equilibrium of the other.

Good parents are always trying to achieve a delicate balance between careful guidance and sympathetic enjoyment of a child. At one and the same time we must nurture the values and virtues we believe will make our children both good and happy, and take pleasure in their growing independence and discovery of their own gifts and enthusiasms. I suspect that the majority of parents err on the side of having too many rules, plans, and ambitions for their children and too little sympathetic enjoyment.

Ultimately, the greatest gift we can give our children, our friends, or our lovers is to support and celebrate their own unfolding sense of purpose, vocation, and joy in living.

∝✗∽

The Practice of Enjoyment

✧ Imagine how many people at the moment are attending weddings, dancing for joy, making love, celebrating the birth of a child, being reunited with an old friend, playing in surf, singing, creating a life work, and so on.

✧ As you go through the day, become a spy in the kingdom of joy. Look for signs that strangers you meet are enjoying themselves, and actually or vicariously join them.

✧ Take a child to the circus, and enjoy the contact high.

✧ Send an anonymous gift to someone you find difficult, and imagine the pleasure he or she will get on receiving it.

✧ Take a series of empathic forays into the lives of your child, your lover, your mate, and your most intimate friend. First, ask each of them what they most enjoy about themselves. Next, try to place yourself within the pride and pleasure they get from being themselves.

CARE:
Responsible Action

❧

Once when Care was crossing a river she saw some clay; she thoughtfully took up a piece and began to shape it. While she was meditating on what she had made, Jupiter came by. Care asked him to give it spirit, and this he gladly granted. But when she wanted her name to be bestowed upon it, he forbade this, and demanded that it be given his name instead. While Care and Jupiter were disputing, Earth arose and desired that her own name be conferred on the creature, since she had furnished it with part of her body. They asked Saturn to be their arbiter, and he made the following decision, which seemed a just one: "Since you, Jupiter, have given its spirit, you shall receive that spirit at its death; and since you, Earth, have given its body, you shall receive its body. But since Care first shaped this creature, she shall possess it as long as it lives. And because there is now a dispute among you as to its name, let it be called 'homo,' for it is made out of humus (earth)."

—MARTIN HEIDEGGER, *BEING AND TIME*

We are ultimately at home in the world not through dominating or explaining or appreciating, but through caring and being cared for.

—MILTON MAYEROFF, *ON CARING*

Scene: *Remembering Care*

As a child I lived within a circle of care that left me with rich memories of sacramental gestures and nurturance hidden within acts of simple kindness and daily succor.

I remember trays of graham cracker ice cream that cooled the tongue on sultry summer afternoons, and cups of steaming cocoa with marshmallows floating on top that took away the chill from sledding too long on winter nights.

I remember the hours Mother bundled her brood into a single bed and read to us—missionary stories that we endured and *The Hardy Boys* that we savored.

I remember the Bible reading, the family prayers, the endless hours in Sunday school, Christian Endeavor, and church that gave me an abiding sense that the world is an arena for soulmaking and marked me with an anxious concern for my salvation.

I remember the support I received for my changing dreams of becoming an ornithologist, a rancher, a philosopher.

I remember the gift of the paintings of John James Audubon and the binoculars Granny helped me buy, so I could pursue my passion for birds.

I remember the time my father drove me a thousand miles to Cornell University, walked into the office of Dr. Arthur A. Allen, announced that I wanted to become an ornithologist, and asked the foremost authority on birds in the world to show me around his laboratory.

I remember the books about dehorning and castrating steers and the care of horses that my mother requested from the unbelieving librarian in Wilmington, Delaware.

I remember teachers and professors I encountered when I abandoned the faith of my fathers, who recognized and cherished my questioning mind and challenged me to wrestle with

Kierkegaard, Kant, and Camus and discover the path to my own truth.

SCENE: *Anonymous Care*

Once in a restaurant in Santa Fe, I watched a man as he watched a poorly dressed woman and child eating breakfast at another table. When he had finished his meal, he went to the cashier, paid his bill and that of the woman and child, and left without a word.

DOING LOVE: *Active Caring*

Care moves love from feeling into action, from self to other, from getting to giving. When we care, we take responsibility for and seek the well-being and fulfillment of another person; our capacity for empathy, compassion, and sympathetic enjoyment is mobilized on behalf of a child, a friend, a lover, a stranger in distress.

Caring liberates us from the self-encapsulation of modern individualism, where "I do my thing, you do your thing," and it carries us beyond the sweet spontaneity and intoxication of the romantic adrenaline-endorphin cocktail into the realm of consideration and thoughtfulness.

There are two great wellsprings that feed our impulse to care—the spirit of generosity and the call to compassion.

At times we feel so blessed by the very existence of our child, our friend, our lover, our mate, that our hearts overflow with spontaneous gratitude. The gift they bestow on us by their presence, the vicarious joy we experience in sharing their lives, elicits a great sigh of thanksgiving and with it a desire to please, help, and delight them in any way we can. Suddenly we are inhabited by a generosity of spirit—what Aristotle called magnanimity, or largeness of soul—that causes us to be concerned for their happiness. We feel the union of I and thou; we love our neighbor as our self. And we give for the pure joy of it. Likewise, recollecting and giving thanks for the myriad ways in which we have been the recipients of care from parents, family, friends, lovers, and strangers stimulates generosity.

Compassion also makes the soul pregnant with a desire to care but in a different manner. When we dare to feel and identify with our fellow-beings, their tragedy, disease, pain, loneliness, or homelessness reaches us as a cry for help—a vocation. We are called to take responsibility for doing what is in our power to alleviate their suffering.

Care-giving covers a range from massaging the sore muscles of a lover to sending money to Save the Children, from tender touch to sweet charity. It often involves taking responsibility for those who can't or won't take responsibility for themselves—a child, a parent with Alzheimer's, a lover or friend who has fallen ill, refugees in a war-torn land.

THE DEGRADATION OF CARE

Currently, there is an immense confusion about the relationship between love and care. In the degree that we take our model of love from romance, we stress excitement and desire rather than responsibility and care-giving as its central ingredients. When this happens, we tend to think of care-giving as a burden that, unfortunately, comes with long-term commitments. Somewhere along the way the modern mind has ambushed and degraded the notion of care.

As a philosophical detective, one of the tricks I use to find out what is happening in the invisible realms of an era's psyche and spirit is to chart what happens to certain key words. Notice the emphasis and tone of the following definitions of *care*. *The Oxford English Dictionary* defines it as: "1. Mental suffering, sorrow, grief, trouble. 2. Burdened state of mind arising from fear, doubt or concern about anything: solicitude. 3. Serious or grave attention; the charging of the mind with anything; concern, heedfulness. 4. Charge; oversight with a view to protection, preservation, guidance." *Microsoft Word Finder* lists the synonyms of *care: affliction, alarm, anxiety, apprehension, consternation, dismay, dread, fear, fright, horror, ordeal, panic, terror, trepidation, trial, trouble, worry, advisement, conference, consultation, counsel, attention, awareness, carefulness, cognizance, concern.* The metamessage contained in both these definitions is: "Care is mostly a drag, an ordeal to be avoided if possible." There is no hint that it may be "more blessed to give than to receive," that much of the meaning of our lives is created by tending, nurturing, and taking responsibility for the well-being of others.

Is it any wonder, with these associations attached to the idea of care, that we have transferred as much as possible of our responsibility for succoring, tending, educating, and healing to the "caring professions"—care-sellers? We have created child-care specialists, teachers, social workers, physicians, nurses, psychotherapists, ministers, and morticians who, for a price, do for us what neighbors once did for each other.

As neighborhoods and communities have been destroyed under the onslaught of our deracinating style of life, the professionalization of care has become a lamentable expedient. Our American ideal of radical individualism, our constant moving from one place to another in the pursuit of upward mobility, our systematic destruction of family and communal bonds, means that most of us are educated by teachers who know little about us, and that we are tended in sickness and dying by strangers whose availability has been determined by the accountants of managed health care delivery systems.

Happily, generosity and real care-giving often survive the bureaucratic hazards and temptations to callousness to which care-sellers are prey. Yesterday I visited my old friend Jim in the hospital, two days after his open-heart quadruple-bypass surgery. Throughout the day I watched one young male nurse with a growing sense of admiration. As he attended to the myriad needs of his patients—washing, changing bandages, making beds—he refused to allow the quantity of the demands placed on him to affect the quality of his care. He took his time with every patient, was exquisitely present, listening, responding, and comforting. Clearly he was not doing a job, was not performing a duty, but was expressing his vocation—giving of himself. By contrast, a dietitian with a clipboard came into the room with a cool swish of starched efficiency in response to Jim's repeated requests for different food. She made little effort to suggest alternatives and had to be reminded twice that her clipboard contained the information that Jim was allergic to lactose and gluten. A sickening care-seller.

If we believe that the deepest satisfaction possible in life comes from loving and being loved, we need to redeem the notion of care and understand its relationship to the other elements of love. Love without care is reduced to a trivial sentiment or a momentary lust.

SKILLFUL CARE

Our feelings of generosity and our desire to care do not automatically translate into wisdom. A large part of the practice of love involves knowing what to give to whom. Care-giving is complex and may be hazardous. Like buoys on a reef, two popular maxims warn of some of the dangers: "No good deed goes unpunished," and "If things don't get better soon, I may have to ask you to stop helping me." Chicken soup may cure a cold or poison us. A gift may be an instrument of grace that empowers its recipient or a disguised weapon that cripples. Questionable motives may trigger seemingly care-ful acts. A gift or a helpful act may be a way to produce dependency, to create obligation, to affirm superiority, to defuse criticism or hostility, or to avoid giving time, presence, and vulnerability.

I have a friend who is a chronic hypochondriac. His wife caters to his every symptom. If his stomach is too delicate for the fish she has prepared, she makes him broth. If he is chilly because there is a draft coming from somewhere, she fetches him a sweater. If he feels he might have a cold coming on, she cancels her plans and stays home with him. If he is too upset to drive into the city, she chauffeurs him and waits around for him to do his errands. The more she helps, the more his mysterious ailments become the focus of their life. Hopeless helping.

Beware of helping! Beware of not helping!

All of us who are parents (or were raised by parents) understand that there is often a poor fit between the gift and the need. We give too little or too much, too soon or too late. We invade our children with our anxieties and ambitions, are over-solicitous when we should step back and allow them to experience the thrill and threat of freedom, are indulgent when we should discipline, neglectful when we should attend to their changing sense of self. We give them clothes, cash, and cars when what they need is confrontation, conversation, and companionship.

It takes time and wisdom to know how to give in a nonintrusive, creative way, to nurture the best in another person. A seasoned lover develops what Buddhism calls "the skillful means" to express compassion in an effective way. To do this involves the practice of empathy, the effort to inhabit another's biography and imagine how he or she sees and experiences the world. It is only from *within* such an empathetic reconstruction that we can figure out what kind of help, care, gifts are relevant.

Although caring always involves a willingness and intention to act, sometimes the best thing we can do is be present to another person's struggle, suffering, and hope. One of the most powerful forms of caring for the young is holding the dream of who they might become in trust for them until they are powerful enough to claim it as their own. As we sometimes inspire others by our example, we may *enhope* them by the vision we have of their potentialities and promise. Often a parent or teacher sees a child's talents and gifts long before the child is aware of them. We need to re-mind each other of who we may yet become.

Even at its best, care-giving in an intimate and familial setting raises a host of difficult questions with which each of us must live. How much should I sacrifice of my time, my priorities, my interests, my energy, my money to care for others? When does self-sacrifice become a form of self-negation? If I neglect the cultivation of my gifts, the nurturing of my deepest needs, the enjoyment of those pleasures that tickle my peculiar fancy, it is unlikely that my caring for others will spring from the bounty of my being. Whenever we abandon our personal sense of vocation and joie de vivre, we place an enormous burden on others to justify the sacrifices we have made "for their sake." The only rule of thumb I know is: Avoid either/or, embrace both/and. Develop those modes of caring that allow you to love both self and others. The sacrifices love demands of us should make our lives rich in meaning and satisfaction.

The Tragic Limits of Care

Once our compassion is awakened, we face a tragic dilemma. The quantity of human need is infinite, but our ability to offer care is finite. Each of us has limited resources, time, energy, and attention to give to others. Thus, when we choose to care for some, we necessarily neglect others. More often than not, we find ourselves *caring about* persons we are unable *to take care of* in any material way. These days, the miracle of television has brought an overwhelming quantity of violence, anarchy, and suffering into our living rooms. Multitudes of refugees fleeing scenes of ethnic slaughter, whole populations living in squalor and hopeless poverty, come by satellite with our morning toast and tea. Seemingly the only gross world product that increases every year is suffering. As the rich, the powerful, and the privileged elite enjoy a cornucopia of goods and services, the masses in the "underdeveloped" countries live in conditions of escalating privation, poverty, and powerlessness. Mere awareness of the situation tempts us to turn our eyes away, deaden our empathy, and harden our hearts so we will not feel impotent.

In the face of the infinite quantity of human need, how is it possible to continue to care without falling into despair?

It is only when we begin to face the impossibility of eliminating suffering and tragedy from the human condition that we discover the link between faith, hope, and love. To be a lover means to refuse to despair and to decide to care even when it breaks the heart. In the final analysis caring is not so much a matter of doing good works as it is the gift of attention and concern to another, whether or not there is anything we can do.

Care is a stone thrown into a sea of suffering that sends ripples out in widening concentric circles.

The smallest circle encompasses the self. The complex relationship between me, myself, and I must be marked by that same "kindly and sympathetic disposition to aid the needy or suffering" with which I approach a friend or a stranger.

Expanding the circumference, the heart goes out to care for those within the field of intimacy, in which our lovers, family, and friends dwell.

Beyond the hearth, we offer hospitality, civility, services, and our talents to members of our immediate community and strangers who cross our path.

At the outer edge of our sphere of care lie the multitude of exiles, homeless, poor, undernourished, sick, war-torn peoples whom we never encounter in the flesh. These we touch by charity: taking action at a distance to improve the condition of persons we do not know, by sharing our surplus wealth and encouraging political policies that will create greater justice, peace, and opportunity.

Beyond the human community is the commonwealth of sentient beings with whom we share this planet and to whom we owe respect and protection.

It is only when we live at the intersection, where the ripples of care that originate in countless individual hearts meet, that this wild, wonderful, and terrifying world becomes a home.

❧

THE PRACTICE OF CARE

❖ Begin your practice by remembrance and thanksgiving. Recollect the history of care that has brought you to this point in your life. Start with your earliest memories of your family, and continue up to the present.

✧ How did your father and mother express their care for you? Cuddling, playing, conversing, preparing special meals, helping with homework, giving gifts, going on fishing trips?

✧ In what ways did you feel neglected, unwanted, uncared for, a latchkey kid, a nuisance to busy parents?

✧ Who beyond the circle of your family cared for you as a child and as a grown person?

✧ How wide and inclusive or narrow and exclusive is the circle of those for whom you care? Does it extend beyond your family and friends? Whose body do you care for? What land? What organizations? What community?

✧ Who falls outside your circle of care?

✧ What special gifts do you have that are needed by others? In what forms of care are you most skillful, efficient, and creative? How do you express care? By touching, tending, teaching, healing, listening, mentoring, giving advice, giving money?

✧ Imagine that a documentary filmmaker followed you around for a week and filmed your every act of care. What would the film show you doing?

STORYTELLING:
The Loving Narrative

But intimate time was not just lived and lost, it was converted into the story Chloe and I told ourselves about ourselves, the self-referential narrative of our love. With its roots in the epic tradition, love is necessarily tied to the tale (to speak of love always involves narrative), and more particularly, to adventure, structured by clear beginnings, endings, goals, reversals and triumphs.
—ALAIN DE BOTTON, *ON LOVE*

SCENE: *A Love Story My Mother Told to Me*

"In the winter of 1937 you children had endless colds and Lawrence was just recovering from pneumonia, so your dad and I decided I should take you to Florida for a few months. Dad had to stay in Tennessee to work, and we had never been apart for very long. We had been in Florida for about a month when I got a package from him that contained a couple dozen large-size medicine capsules with the instruction that I was to open one a day. In each capsule he had put a note that contained a word or two that referred to some place or person or event that had been important to us. I still have some of the notes, and I thought you might enjoy them.

"*Scotch plaid and a sailor hat.* This refers to a time when Dad was twenty-one and I was eleven and I accompanied him on the piano when he played the violin. On this particular occasion he and I and a college girl who played with him went away overnight to do a concert. My mother made me a Scotch plaid pleated skirt and a red satin jacket and bought me a sailor hat. We had a wonderful time on that trip, and that was the time I announced to the people we were staying with that I was going to marry Mr. Keen when I grew up. And eight years later I did.

"*Pete Hurth's car.* Pete Hurth was a railroad executive, and he had a private car that he sometimes lent my parents. One time we went up to Calderwood, and they parked the car on a siding, and we spent several days there. Every day the train would come and hook up to us and give us heat and electricity. In the morning we woke up to cowbells. That was an unforgettable place for me because, at the time, I was wearing a boy's fraternity pin, and your dad came up, and we went out for a moonlight walk, and I lost it. It took a little explanation to tell the boy why I couldn't give him back his pin.

"*Robert E. Lee Hotel.* When I was in Salem College, I spent one weekend with the woman who later married your uncle Sam. Dad picked me up on Monday morning and drove me back to college. We stopped at the Robert E. Lee Hotel to have breakfast, which was a very daring thing to do in 1927, and the college authorities were very displeased with me.

"*A rose jar.* When I was in college, your dad sent me a wrist corsage every Saturday, and for years I kept the petals from all the corsages in a jar.

"*Mrs. Keen.* When we were first married, we spent a week or two in a friend's cabin. An old country lady who lived nearby told us we could catch a chicken and cook it, and she also gave us various things to eat, which was fortunate because I had never cooked before. When we first met her, Dad said, 'Aunt

Lolly, this is my wife, Mrs. Keen.' Nobody had called me Mrs. Keen before, and I was so proud I nearly died.

"*The ocean.* I had never seen the ocean until your dad took me to Rehoboth Beach, Delaware. The waves knocked me down when we went swimming, and I got to my feet and said, 'This water has something in it.' And of course it did—salt.

"*Redwood forest.* On my first trip to the West Coast, we drove through the redwood forest very slowly. When we had looked and looked and looked till we couldn't look anymore, we stopped the car. Dad got out and climbed on the top of the car—it was a station wagon with a flat roof—and lay down and had me drive so he could see the trees.

"*Hiccups.* We brought Lawrence home from the hospital when he was two weeks old, and he got hiccups, and we were terrified. So we called our friend Dr. Ellis to ask him what to do. He assured Dad that hiccups were perfectly normal, and then he said: 'Alvin, be sure to call me when the baby wets his diaper.'

"*Kasha soup.* Once when I became very ill with blood poisoning, I was too sick to eat. When I began to get better, Dad drove sixteen miles over to Knoxville to get me a carton of kasha soup, which was my favorite food.

"*St. John's Mountain.* At Sunshine, on the top of the mountain, there was a very secluded place where leaves and pine needles had fallen from the trees and formed a thick carpet that was warmed by the sun. Dad and I made love there.

"There are a lot of other capsules that contain the names of very dear friends with whom we spent many happy hours. And there are several that are about things the two of us shared that I want to keep private."

SCENE: *A Story Lost*

Whenever I think about the comforts of a shared story, I hear the sad voice of an old college friend who recently told me about the pain he has each day as he spoon-feeds his wife, who has Alzheimer's disease and can no longer remember his name or any of the rich history they have shared for fifty years.

THE BIOMYTHIC ANIMAL

Human beings are storytellers. Our being is inseparable from our telling. The way our brains are formed and function and our biochemistry are inseparable from our values, choices, worldviews, and myths (and the social-political institutions that reflect them). Quite literally our myths in-form our bodyminds. We create the brain as much as it creates us. What distinguishes us from the higher apes is not our capacity to make tools but the strange way in which our narratives about who we are in-form our biology. In the strictest sense of the word, human beings, unlike dolphins or our near kin the higher apes, are not biological animals. Until we have stories to in-form us, we do not know what to eat, how to spend our days, or how, when, and with whom to mate. Our myths about food, sexuality, and warfare both shape and alter our appetites, desires, and aggressive impulses.

Animals live in a natural landscape; humans inhabit a fabricated storyscape.

Love me, love my story. Human intercourse is an intermingling of flesh and story, not a mere joining of bodies. In love, the telling and the touching are two sides of the same coin. In warfare and casual sex, we reduce the other to a biological object, a body without a history or a hope. To fondle, conquer, or possess the bodies of others without entering into the story of their lives is a violation of our essential humanity. Anonymous sex, scoring, and body counts are only differing degrees of desecration.

Falling in love, we talk, listen, and become the intimate audience for the narratives that we have so far dramatized only within the solitary theater of our self-consciousness. If we persist in the quest for love and knowledge, we become each other's historians and biographers. Over the years it takes to create a friendship or a marriage, we listen to each other's stories so often that our autobiographies become inscribed in each other's hearts. Finally, what we call love becomes inseparable from knowing and being known.

One of the most formative experiences of my life was the discovery that nothing opened my heart so surely as listening to stories that people told me about their lives. I am by nature reserved, a recovering Presbyterian given to critical analysis and stern judgment in the tradition of John Calvin. When I started conducting seminars in personal mythology and autobiography thirty years ago, I found that I first became interested, then empathic, and finally compassionate, as I learned more and more about the details of a person's life. I believe, with Henry Wadsworth Longfellow, that "if we could read the secret history of our enemies, we should find in each person's life sorrow and suffering enough to disarm all hostility." Telling and listening, sharing our life stories, is the most powerful method we have for increasing the quantity of love in the world.

Human beings alone "make" love. Other animals may engage in sensuous play, copulate, bond, and perhaps express affection. But they lack the crucial element that allows love to transcend the purely biological realm—dramatic language. Because we tell stories and understand and define who we are only by placing ourselves within a narrative, we are the only bio-mythic animals. (Ergo: Books that reduce love to chemistry, and sex to techniques for stimulation, should be addressed to our chimpanzee cousins, who have learned to use simple tools but as yet haven't discovered how to prolong orgasms.)

Love Stories and Hate Stories

For better and for worse, humankind is molded by the various stories we tell about ourselves. Our stories govern who, when, where, how, and why we love or hate, nurture or destroy, caress or torture. Just as making war involves creating an elaborate political drama of good versus evil that transforms a neighbor into an enemy, making love involves creating an elaborate story that transforms strangers into friends, accidental acquaintances into star-crossed lovers. Every plural entity—a friendship, a pair of lovers, a marriage, a family, a community—is bound together by the creation of a shared story.

To understand how we make love by making stories, let's imagine the differences between the ways a propagandist, a biographer, and a lover might tell a story that has dominated the news—the assassination of Yitzhak Rabin, prime minister of Israel.

Yigal Amir, the assassin, a member of a right-wing religious sect—as is usually the case with ideologues and religious fanatics—viewed his target not as a man but as "the enemy." His Rabin was a caricature drawn in a moralistic, black-and-white monotone—*nothing but* an enemy of God, a Nazi, a non-Jewish Jew who, by acting in defiance of the biblical justification for settling the occupied West Bank and Gaza Strip, was creating a terrorist state that endangered the lives of real Jews. Armed with a story that reduced Rabin to an abstraction, a symbol of evil, Amir could kill him and proclaim with a self-righteous conscience untouched by compassion, "I acted alone on God's orders, and I have no regrets."

Future biographers of Rabin will have to go beneath the facade of politics and propaganda, the abstractions, the official story, and enter deeply into the complexities of the life and times of the man. With as much information as they can collect, as much empathy as they can marshal, honest biographers will trace the line of coherence that links the warrior who was a commander in the Jewish underground at the birth of Israel and survived three subsequent wars to the diplomat who finally shook hands with his archenemy Yasir Arafat and won the Nobel peace prize. It is easy to imagine that the portrait that emerges will be rich in ambiguity and paradox and will contain accounts of the agonizing decisions and the multicolored hopes that marked Rabin's historical destiny.

Finally, let us imagine the story that might be told by Rabin's widow, Leah. For her, it is not the prime minister, the man of destiny, who has been assassinated, but her husband, her lover, the father of her children, the companion of her years. Because it is of the essence of the most complete love stories to remain private, we can only guess what she might tell. Certainly she will remember their first meeting, falling in love and growing in marriage, their shared jokes, their struggles, the smell of the man, the texture of his skin, the secrets of the bedroom. Without question, the intimate details of their marriage and their shared memories and hopes are too numerous and complex to be summed up. The years of accumulated knowledge, desire, empathy, compassion, respect, and commitment will have left her with a unique story that she and Yitzhak created together about a man nobody but she ever knew—or loved—so well.

The differences among these three—the hate story, the official story, and the love story—give us some clues about how the stories we weave decrease or increase our capacity for love.

A hate story automatically reduces a person to a label, a stereotype, a member of a despised group. When we approach someone with our prejudices intact, we ignore the richness and complexity of the individual—a person with a name, a face, a history—and assign him or her to an a priori category, a box, from which there is no escape. He is *nothing but* a Jew, an Arab, a nigger, a honky, a slant, a greaser—an enemy. Nothing is so predictable or monotonous as the hate story because it thrives only when we conspire to ignore the odd and interesting, lovely and troublesome details that characterize the life of every individual and when we refuse to exercise empathy and compassion. Both political propaganda and the personal hate story follow the same formula; I am right, you are wrong; I am innocent, you are to blame; I am human, you are subhuman. The less we know, the more easily we hate.

An official story is told from the perspective of a narrator who attempts to remain objective. The narrator, like any responsible biographer, must be knowledgeable and empathetic. He or she will collect as much information as possible in an attempt to understand, reconstruct, explain, and make an informed judgment about the historical importance of the subject of the story. A good biographer or journalist may admire or despise the subject of the story but will make every effort to be fair and comprehensive.

In a love story the central characters are so intertwined that objectivity is impossible. As love grows from acquaintance to commitment with the accumulation of common experience, sharing of memories, and hopes, two bodies become one flesh, two autobiographies are woven into a single complex story, two monologues are fused into a living dialogue.

One measure of love is the degree to which the beloved escapes our categories, transcends our understanding, and evades our explanations—those habits of mind that, like cookie cutters, stamp people into the simplistic shapes of lions or lambs, good or bad, kind or cruel, strong or weak, masculine or feminine. The more we love, the less we can reduce someone (or ourselves) to a formula or an explanation of twenty or twenty-five thousand words. The light of respect reveals facet upon facet of the diamond, of the person, that is concealed from the objective eye. The angle of admiration places us in a perspective from which we see so much that we become mute before the complexity, the ambiguity, and the paradox of the beloved.

If you ask me if my love is like a summer day, I would reply: "Yes. She is like a sultry Kansas afternoon, charged with flash lightning, tense with waiting for the rain; and like a winter morning when the fire melts the frost on the windowpane. She is mean as a menstruating rattlesnake that strikes without warning, and kind as a mother who nurses a sick child through exhausting nights. And, and, and . . ." I could add metaphors and descriptions without end, and I still would not have captured her in the web of language.

Sometimes at the gathering of family and friends following a funeral, you can hear a bountiful collection of stories that are a spontaneous testimony to the complex beauty of the deceased. Usually the official eulogy tries to praise but succeeds only in sanitizing the dead. It is not until after the ceremony, at the funeral feast, that the true celebration begins. "I remember one time when Buck got in a fight with one of the meanest of the McKinley boys. They went at it till they were both beat up pretty good, and Buck got that old boy in a kind of bear hold where he couldn't move, and he damn near squeezed the life out of him. Then he just held him there till he quit fighting, and by God, if he didn't kiss that boy right on the cheek and let him go and walk away. He could be one tough son-of-a-bitch." "That's true. But did you ever see him gentle a horse? Once I saw him buy a little roan colt over at the auction that had been abused by someone and was skitterish and half out of his mind with fear. Well, Buck took a couple handfuls of oats and put them in his coat pocket and climbed over the fence and sat in the corner of the pen. And he just waited while that colt looked wild-eyed at him and pushed himself against the opposite corner trying to get as far away as he could. But Buck just sat still and held the oats in his hand. I don't know how long it took, but when I came back after dark, you would have thought them two was having a love affair. He was petting that colt all over, and the colt was smelling him and licking his hand. You never could tell what Buck was going to do, could you?"

Ludwig Mies van der Rohe said of great architecture, "God lives in the details." The same can be said of great love. Lovers come to inhabit a storyscape filled with shared memories of Scotch plaid skirts and pine forests and other private tokens of intimacy.

Love may begin as a feeling of desire or compassion, but it rapidly escapes from the immediacy of the present and extends its dominion over the future and the past by weaving memories and hopes and ongoing interactions into a coherent narrative.

When we first meet someone, there is nothing to remember and no thought of the future. But gradually love creates from shared memory and expectation a common past and a common future, a story that reaches back and forward in time.

The house of memory any couple builds is constructed from the blended remembrances of both. The story my wife and I share now contains all the cast of characters that were originally separated. Her biological father (who left before she was born), her daddy, mother, grandfather, grandmother, brother, friends, and former lovers interact with my father, mother, brother, sisters, friends, and former lovers to create a complex plot.

LOVE-TALK: *Dialogue and Communion*

Although bi-autobiographies are always complex, the primary stuff of which they are made is simple—uninhibited conversation and unending dialogue. Love is the original and only enduring free speech movement. It unlocks the tongue, allows us to talk about anything, creates wholesome speech. The truth, the whole truth, and nothing but the truth is never told in court. It can only be spoken within a sanctuary created by those who care for each other unconditionally.

So much for theory. In fact, it is very difficult for most of us to tell the truth, the whole truth, and nothing but the truth to (1) ourselves, (2) our parents, (3) our children, (4) our lover and/or spouse, (5) our friends, (6) our therapist or minister, (7) our boss, customer, tax accountant, and miscellaneous other associates, (8) strangers. Ideally, at the far end of the rainbow, love, trust, and truth are inseparable. I have yet to arrive at such a place myself, but it is the destination toward which I travel. I find that one way I can measure whether I am making any progress on the path of love is to mark my (hopefully growing) willingness to risk telling the truth to any or all of the above.

It is helpful to remember that honest dialogue always involves a confrontation between thesis and antithesis before a synthesis can evolve. Therefore, a love story is likely to be more a saga of an ongoing wrestling match than a description of a perfectly graceful dance—Fred Astaire and Ginger Rogers. The harmonics of love emerge from clash–come together–move apart–clash–come together–move apart–ad infinitum. In the background of love you can detect the clanging of armor, the crunching of egos, the war of the roses. The world according to love is made from yes and no. Dialogue, not war, is the father and mother of all things. The philosopher Karl Jaspers said that any dialogue is a form of "loving combat." Thus, one of the best arguments for love is that the best arguments, the most honest dialogue, can take place only between lovers.

Over the course of time a true love story will undergo constant revision in mood and mode. Because every enduring relationship is destined to confront the inevitable joys and sufferings of the human condition, the narrative of love can never end with a superficial "and they lived happily ever after." It must be cast in all the classical forms in which stories are told—romance, tragedy, irony, and comedy. It will be a Technicolor tale that includes longing, struggle, frustration, ecstasy, pleasure, pain, betrayal, fidelity, alienation, reconciliation, loneliness, communion, folly, wisdom, and every human emotion. So long as we remain in communion, we will always be in the process of co-authoring a never-ending story.

Beloved: Weave a world with me. Abandon constraint. Speak boldly and listen carefully, until our words and silence entwine to form a single gnarled story. Let us share memories: of enchanted and terrible childhoods, fathers and mothers who were large as giants and faithful, fickle, and foolish in their omnipotent love; of enemies, betrayals, casualties, raw hatred, battles won and lost, and wounds that have scarcely healed; of dark journeys into regions of hell where hungry spirits and demons still remind us of ancient guilt and senseless shame; of friends, companions, guides, and healing spirits. Let us dare to speak of our abiding dreams and occasional visions, and of the endless longing for some sanctuary beside the still waters where the soul can rest within the everlasting arms of the Soulmaker.

⤫

THE PRACTICE OF LOVE STORIES

All the people who have loved you and whom you have loved are linked in the intricate story you tell yourself and others about your life. Father, mother, brothers, sisters, grandparents, friends, lovers, mates, ex-mates, take on the roles of faithful heroes and betraying villains, saints and fools, helpers and rascals.

✧ Who are the central characters—faithful and false lovers and friends—in your amorous autobiography?

✧ Do you tell your love stories as tragic tales of fated relationships in which you were the victim, as heroic romances in which love conquers all, as ironic episodes that prove we should not expect too much, as comedies in which fools loved and won or lost but never wisely?

✧ What characters are included in the bi-autobiography you create with your most intimate partner? Who is in your thermonuclear family, the expanded circle of relationships that makes up the memory bank and community you share—his and her parents, his ex-wife, her children by a previous marriage, Great-uncle Albert, whose fortune you inherited, the lingering ghosts of former lovers, a circle of friends, various enemies?

In the love story two people create over time, familiarity may breed contempt or contentment. The old stories may become as boring and stale as old jokes. Or revisiting a common past may become a part of the liturgy of relationship that is as pleasurable as the often-repeated dance of sexual communion.

✧ What stories of triumphant and betrayed love have been repeated so often in your family, your marriage, among your circle of friends, that they are like polished stones? Which delight and which bore you?

✧ One measure of love is the degree to which it unlocks the tongue, allows us to talk about anything, creates wholesome speech. Where are you tongue-tied? What of great importance do you not talk about? What inner dialogues do you habitually have that you do not share? What are the unfinished conversations in your life? What would you like to say to your father, mother, brother, sister, lover, child?

REPENTING:
Forgiving and Renewal

And forgive us our debts,
As we also have forgiven our debtors.
                    —THE GOSPEL ACCORDING
                       TO MATTHEW

O look, look in the mirror,
    O look in your distress;
Life remains a blessing
    Although you cannot bless.

O stand, stand in the window
    As the tears scald and start.
You shall love your crooked neighbor
    With your crooked heart.
                            —W. H. AUDEN

The Eleventh Commandment: "Thou shalt not b/lame!"

SCENE: *A Friend's Laments*

"Long ago and far away, I expected love to be light and easy and without failure.

"Before we moved in together, we negotiated a prenuptial agreement. Neither of us had been married before, and we were both involved in our separate careers. So our agreement not to have children suited us both. Until . . . on the night she announced that her period was late and she was probably pregnant, we both treated the matter as an embarrassing accident with which we would have to deal. Why us? Why now? Without much discussion, we assumed we would do the rational thing—get an abortion. As the time approached, she began to play with hypothetical alternatives, to ask in a plaintive voice with half misty eyes: 'Maybe we should keep the baby. Maybe we could get a live-in helper, and it wouldn't interrupt our lives too much. Maybe I could even quit my job and be a full-time mother for a few years. Maybe . . .' To each *maybe* I answered: 'Be realistic. Neither of us is willing to make the sacrifices to raise a child.' She allowed herself to be convinced, silenced the voice of her irrational hopes and dreams, and terminated the pregnancy.

"It has been many years now since our 'decision,' and we are still together and busy with our careers and our relationship. Still no children, even though we have recently been trying to get pregnant. I can't help noticing that she suffers from spells of regret and guilt, and a certain mood of sadness settles over her. At times I know she longs for her missing child and imagines what he or she would be doing now. I reassure her that we did the right thing. But when I see her lingering guilt and pain and her worry that she missed her one chance to become a mother, I feel that I failed an important test of love. Because my mind had been closed to anything that would interrupt my plans for the future, I had listened to her without deep empathy or compassion. I'm no longer sure we made the right decision. I am sure that in refusing to enter into her agony, to share the pain of her ambivalence, I betrayed her.

"I have asked for and, I think, received forgiveness, but there remains a scar that was caused by my insensitivity and self-absorption."

BROKEN AND DIRTY: *Love Among the Fragments*

If romance is the dream of the idealized self, the ongoing practice of repentance and forgiveness is the highest achievement of the actual self.

One of the more seductive notions to emerge out of pop psychology is the New Age ideal of post-therapeutic love. The story goes something like this: He and She were both battle-scarred veterans of marriages and/or significant relationships that failed because of immaturity, addiction, co-dependence, or the unwillingness of one or both partners to "grow" and develop their full potential. After much struggle and divorce, He and She entered therapy and/or embarked on a spiritual path, worked on themselves, and finally "got it all together." One enchanted evening the paths of these two self-actualized, autonomous persons crossed, and they formed a fully mature, nondependent, mutually supportive partnership and lived harmoniously ever after.

Don't count on it. Somewhere over the rainbow there may be loving dyads that bask in the sunlight of perpetual high noon, that cast no shadow, that are unmarked by darkness. But if such angelic lovers exist, I have yet to meet them. I have, however, encountered many authentic Heroes and Sheroes of love, men and women who have struggled with abuse, cruelty, indifference, fear, paranoia, addiction, and greed and became wise and compassionate in the process. As nearly as I can tell, the secret of these extraordinary lovers is that they became experts in repentance and forgiveness.

To be human is to be flawed, faulted, a fragment of what we might ideally become. Because we are born naked and helpless and survive only if we are nurtured and educated for years by fallible parents and half-sane societies, we are imprinted by the prejudices and myths of family and tribe. In other words, we are twisted by karma or original sin (to use religious language) or are victims of our unconscious (to use the equivalent psychological language). We inevitably begin our life-journey twisted, prejudiced, incomplete, blinded, and egocentric, viewing the world through eyes other than our own. We may come into life "trailing clouds of glory," but by the time we enter adulthood, we are also filled with venom due to the injuries we have sustained in the "normal" process of acculturation.

And so we all begin our quest for love as fragmentary individuals looking for someone with whom we can become whole.

When I was a college freshman, every afternoon I went to the bakery for refreshment and to ogle the succulent young waitress. My budget allowed for only a single oatmeal cookie, a cup of coffee, and a small tip. One day, noticing that I seemed to be lusting after more than I could afford, the waitress of delights and hidden wisdom informed me: "Did you know that for a quarter, instead of buying one whole oatmeal cookie, you could get a bag of brokens and dirties?" "What are brokens and dirties?" I asked. "I'll show you," she said, disappearing into the kitchen and reappearing with a brown bag. Reaching in she took a fragment of a cookie and handed me another. "These are the cookies that came out of the oven in weird shapes or got broken when we took them off the pan."

The real love-feast begins when we discover that a shared bag of brokens and dirties satisfies our appetite much better than a single perfect cookie.

THE ANATOMY OF REPENTANCE

What does it mean to repent?

In a culture like ours, dedicated, on the one hand, to the Enlightenment ideal of rationality, power, triumph, and progress, and addicted, on the other hand, to blame and the new cult of victimhood, repentance is difficult to understand or appreciate.

Let's begin with some large and loose ways of characterizing repentance. To repent is:

to remove the beam from our own eye before trying to take the splinter from the eye of our lover, friend, or neighbor;

to view the self from the perspective of the other;

to embrace our shadow;

to withdraw and reown our projections;

to make conscious our unconscious motivations;

to disarm the defense mechanisms that protect the ego;

to dismantle our character armor;

to move away from false innocence and self-righteousness, or infantile guilt and shame, toward seasoned self-awareness and confession of mature guilt and authentic shame;

to abandon the orientation to blame and claim responsibility for our actions and interactions.

All the great spiritual traditions distinguish two radically different orientations to life. *Ego* is based on the illusion (driven by fear and grasping) that I am the pivot around which everything should revolve. *Spirit* is the awareness that the center is everywhere and that I am a member of a commonwealth of sentient beings, all of whom deserve my compassion. In addition, the spiritual traditions claim that love, along with wisdom, is the only medicine that can cure us of the narcissistic illusions of the ego that alienate us from all other living beings.

We can best appreciate the reorientation involved in repentance by playing with an analogy: The ego is a mini-nation, and egoism is nationalism writ small.

The ego (like a nation) is founded on self-righteousness and defended by propaganda that claims that I (we) am good, innocent, and virtuous while others are aggressive, greedy, and careless. If conflict or warfare erupts, it is because others are malevolent or ignorant. In short, egoism and nationalism are constructed on the principle of paranoia—others (my wife, liberals, the Vietcong, the patriarchy, Saddam Hussein, corporations) are responsible for evil. No matter what horrors they inflict on their neighbors, nations routinely present themselves to the world as well-intentioned victims. After the Second World War, Germany (but not Japan) made some effort to claim responsibility for its aggression and atrocities. Many United States citizens (but few politicians) repented of the policy and actions of our government in Vietnam. But as a rule, nations do not repent.

Enlightened or cruel, benevolent or malevolent, the tyrannical ego insists on its own centrality and imposes its vision of how things were, are, and ought to be on all who live in its ambience. It may control others by fear or favors, but it does not accord them the simple and single dignity upon which love rests—the recognition of the sovereign right of each person to have his or her intimate experience and point of view taken seriously.

Repentance involves a 180-degree turn, a fundamental conversion from ego to spirit, from paranoia to metanoia, from false innocence and blame to reclaiming full responsibility for one's actions. This requires a systematic deconstruction of the "normal" defense mechanisms, motivations, and operating procedures that support the claims of the ego. Instead of proclaiming its innocence, offering excuses, and assigning blame to others, the repentant self claims responsibility for its deeds. Contrary to all the Pollyanna pop psychologists who would liberate us by abolishing guilt, we are never more powerful than when we recognize our complicity in creating suffering, turn away from self-defense, and ask for forgiveness.

The dumbest nine words written about love are: "Love means never having to say you are sorry."

The most powerful nine-word aphrodisiac is: "I was wrong. I am sorry. Please forgive me."

Repentance is hard, get-down-and-get-dirty work. It requires that we become accustomed to a diet of crow, that we acquire the habit of being wrong and saying we are sorry for the myriad injuries we cause. This process never ends.

In love we embrace the gnarled beauty of the self and the other, knowing that we will need to forgive and be forgiven time and again. The best wedding ring is a flawed diamond held secure within a setting of perennial forgiveness.

THE POWER OF FORGIVENESS

Forgiveness is a necessary medicine to heal the wounds we suffer from carelessness and cruelty. In the degree that we refuse to forgive, we are condemned to live with anger and resentment, always seeking an occasion for revenge against those who have wronged us. Once we enter the cycle of resentment and revenge, there is no exit. We are handcuffed to the corpse of a moribund past, locked in an intimate relationship with an enemy who increasingly embitters and poisons us.

The first reason to forgive those who have trespassed against us is not that we are filled with loving kindness but to preserve our own freedom. Resentment keeps the original wound festering. Only forgiveness allows us to put the painful past behind us and create a novel future.

A woman in a seminar shared the story of the moment in her childhood when she discovered the power of forgiveness. "I can't remember now why my father spanked me, but it changed my life. I must have done something that displeased him, but I think he was mad or frustrated about something that didn't have anything to do with me because he spanked me hard, and he had never done that before. I cried and yelled at him, 'I hate you, and I'll never love you again.' He left the room, and I shrank up inside myself and felt small and ashamed, even though I didn't feel like I deserved a spanking. After about an hour he came back into the room and sat on my bed and said, 'I'm sorry.' I could see that he really meant it, and that my words had hurt him, and that my threat not to love him gave me enormous power. My feeling of being small, impotent, and ashamed gave way to the feeling that I had the power to make him suffer by withdrawing my love, or to make him happy by forgiving him. I forgave him. That was the last time he ever spanked me."

Unfortunately, we do not think of power and forgiveness as belonging together. Power is usually narrowly defined as the ability to impose one's will on another. But the result of limiting our concept of power to the ability to triumph in conflict is to create *vicious cycles* of escalating impotence in which manipulation begets manipulation and violence begets violence. Forgiveness alone creates *virtuous cycles*.

The true power of love can be measured by how much we are changed by it. It is folly to set out to change others. Perhaps we can't even change ourselves very much. But the paradox is that within the atmosphere created by forgiveness, we begin to change. In the beginning we want to be completed by love but not changed. We naïvely hope to be appreciated for our faults rather than have them corrected. But in the give-and-take of a long marriage or friendship, when we learn that we are accepted even when we are flawed, ever so gradually we move away from centering the world on our fragile egos. Repenting, forgiving, and being forgiven, we are renewed and given the power to begin again and again.

FORGIVENESS VERSUS ACCEPTANCE

Forgiveness should not be confused with simple forgetting. Often victims of childhood abuse, rape, violence, or torture repress the memories of the brutalizing events but continue to suffer their effects. Before forgiveness can perform the alchemy that releases us from the past, we must allow ourselves to *feel* the full measure of the outrage that has been committed against us *and* hold the guilty party responsible for his or her actions.

Even then it may not be wise or possible to forgive. When we have been injured by someone who will not or cannot repent, someone who is unable or unwilling to take moral responsibility, the best we can do is understand and accept the situation.

I was attending a conference in Scotland when a woman knocked on my door and asked if she could talk to me. "I need to talk to somebody who is not from this village," she explained, "because I don't know how to go about forgiving a local man who raped me." I invited her in and listened to her story. Two years before, she had accepted an invitation to have dinner at the apartment of a local innkeeper. In the course of the evening, he began to make sexual advances, which she rejected politely but firmly—whereupon he overpowered and raped her. Shortly afterward he fell asleep, and she struggled free of his grip and ran away. Since that time she had been haunted by the incident, ashamed that she had been so naïve as to trust the man, enraged that she had been violated, unable to stop the swirl of emotions and memories. Finally she had decided that the only way to reach any closure was to forgive him. "Can I go to him and tell him that I forgive him?" she asked.

"Did you report the incident to the police?" I asked. "No," she replied, "I considered it, but I realized I had no compelling physical evidence to support my charge and was afraid I would be humiliated even more. So I went home and didn't tell anyone."

"Has the man shown any remorse or asked you for forgiveness?" I asked.

"No, I haven't seen him, *and* I have reason to believe that he has done the same thing to other women."

My first instinct was to keep her out of harm's way. "You certainly should not put yourself in danger again by being in the presence of such a man. If you could make contact with any of the other women he has violated, you might file a charge against him even at this late date."

"I don't know any of the other women. And I'm afraid of what people will say if I accuse him after so long a time."

"If any of the other women he raped came forward, would you be willing to add your testimony and hold him accountable for his actions?" I asked. "Yes," she replied.

As we explored the nature of forgiveness, she came to the conclusion that in the circumstances the best she could do to gain a measure of peace was to accept the painful fact that her rapist had no moral sensitivity and that she would be willing to forgive him in the future if he acknowledged that he had wronged her and other women and took responsibility for his actions. Short of that, all she could do was *to refuse to forgive* him and hope that an occasion would arise when he could be forced to face the consequence of his actions.

The story is told in Nicaragua that when Tomás Borges, one of the heroes of the Sandinista revolution, met the man who had earlier tortured him when he was in prison, he said to him, "My revenge is going to be to educate your children."

DISCRIMINATION AND COMPASSIONATE JUDGMENT

In recent years, "Don't be judgmental" has become a byword of those who would reduce love to a sentimental feeling of universal acceptance. Our culture seems to relegate guilt to the junk heap of emotions; we experience it only so long as we have an incomplete understanding of the unconscious motives for our injurious actions. We have come dangerously near to believing that a complete psychoanalysis of Hitler—no doubt he was an abused child in a dysfunctional family—would allow us to forgive him without having to judge him guilty of any willful evil. There is a French proverb that says: "To understand all is to forgive all." But is this true? The psychologist Bruno Bettelheim, who was himself a survivor of the death camps, said that if understanding led automatically to forgiveness, he refused to understand the Nazi commandants because he held them fully responsible for their deeds.

Romance and sentimentality are blind, but mature love is clear-sighted, discriminating, and fair-minded in judgment. Tough love, as practiced in all of the twelve-step programs, demands that we assume responsibility for our actions, repent of our wrongdoing, and make restitution for injuries we have caused before we can expect forgiveness. If we have stolen, we must return the loot. If we have insulted, we must apologize. If we have ignored, we must give attention. If we have committed atrocious crimes, we must find some way to atone for the evil we have done.

One of the things all of us need most in order to grow into fullness is honest feedback, the accurate and compassionate judgment of someone who knows us well.

Intimacy provides us with privileged knowledge and inside information that can enable us to be the best judges of the character and conduct of those we love. Who knows my faults and virtues better than my children, my wife, my friends, the seasoned companions of my years? They know the caves in which I have buried ancient fears and the hollow trees where I have squirreled away secret good deeds. They know my overflowing generosity and my stinginess. They alone have witnessed the rocky soil of my egotism and the long ripening of my compassion. Traces of my anger and neglect, enthusiasm and kindness, are etched on their psyches. They know where I suffer hidden wounds that do not heal. I need their eyes, their loving objectivity, their compassionate judgment. It is to them that I turn when I need true witnesses to help me evaluate my motives and actions.

Judge the people you love honestly and compassionately, and seek their judgment in the hope of creating a community of fair witnesses. Care enough about yourself to make clear judgments, and speak strongly when an offense has been committed against you. Be ready to forgive when you are offered true remorse, and let bygones be bygones.

RITUALS OF REPENTANCE AND RENEWAL

We are always in the process of sending and receiving intricate messages that signal our desire and intention to please or displease, move toward or away from, make love or make war. Our private liturgies of love and hate are deliciously subtle, mutually understood, and objectively unverifiable. The evidence that a gesture of tenderness you made was intended to reestablish ruptured intimacy, or that a "teasing" remark carried a sarcastic barb, can never be proven in a court of law. Intimacy confers on us an unerring knowledge of each other's scars and erogenous zones. You, your lover, spouse, child, parent, friend, all have long fingers that are well educated to push each other's buttons—for better and for worse.

For instance: The emotional climate has been chilly for a long time.

He speaks little unless she asks him a direct question. He is "too busy" to cook the special meal he usually prepares on Wednesday nights.

She works late and "forgets" to make the reservations for the room at the inn by the sea where they were supposed to spend the weekend.

He leaves his sweat clothes on the bathroom floor after she has cleaned the house for a luncheon she is preparing for a couple of her friends.

She slams cupboard doors and turns on the television loud enough to create a decibel overload when he is trying to take a nap.

He avoids eye contact.

She turns sideways (slightly) when they pass in the hall to avoid any semblance of body contact.

They sleep on opposite sides of the bed. Nobody touches.

He sulks.

She sulks.

He seethes.

She seethes.

They pretend nothing is wrong and lead parallel lives in their shared frozen void—for a very long time.

For reasons best known to God, the seasons of the heart do change and winter yields to spring.

Seemingly by accident, twisting and turning in the unconscious darkness, his left foot finds its way across the arctic expanse of bed and comes to rest under the arch of her right foot. "Officially," both remain asleep and take no notice of the restoration of diplomatic relations. Unofficially, both savor the slight indications of a thawing trend and are careful not to disturb the small romance that is afoot.

Come morning, her hand brushes his shoulder as she gets out of bed—ever so casually. "Do you want me to fix some tea and toast?" he asks on his way to the kitchen. "Yes, thank you," she replies without quite acknowledging that he is making an overture toward reconciliation. During a hurried breakfast, several times his eyes focus on her face with an expression that could be interpreted as warm. She notices and responds with what an objective observer might, wrongly, consider a non sequitur: "You look nice this morning." "Thank you," he replies with a trace of a smile. As they converge at the threshold on their way to work, they hazard a chaste kiss good-bye and a parting litany that contains the whisper of a promise: "I'll see you this evening." "Will you be late?" "No, I'll be home about five." "Me too."

When they return at evening rise: It turns out he was just passing the corner bookstore and happened to notice that the book she's been looking for on travel in the Himalayas was in the window, so he bought it for her; and she, it turns out, has bought the makings for creamed chicken on waffles, which he loves because it reminds him of a small country café in which he ate when he was in college. Later in the evening he stands behind her chair and begins to massage the muscles in her shoulders that are always tight. By ten o'clock, they comment that it has been a hard day, and they go to bed, each moving immediately to the center, where the small romance that has been afoot since the night before spreads through the length and breadth of their flesh until they begin to practice the ancient liturgy of touch and mutual delight that they have celebrated together time and time again.

∽⋊∾

THE PRACTICE OF REPENTANCE AND FORGIVENESS

The road that leads through the valley of the shadow is fast, but it can only be taken by those who are willing to practice a heroic measure of self-analysis, self-criticism, and repentance and go directly to the question of their own responsibility for wounding others. For the most part, contemporary psychotherapy follows the slow, indirect road that often does not lead to repentance because it encourages us to discover how we were wounded rather than wounding, how we were victims rather than perpetrators.

I suggest that you, first, attempt the fast road.

✧ Whom have you wronged, betrayed, ignored, injured, manipulated, used?

✧ Where do you feel guilty for what you have done or ashamed for what you have left undone?

✧ For what and from whom do you need forgiveness?

Next, explore the slow road.

✧ Who has wronged, betrayed, ignored, injured, manipulated, used you?

✧ Whom have you forgiven?

✧ What ancient wounds still fester?

✧ What resentments do you still harbor?

✧ What would have to happen for you to forgive those who have trespassed against you?

✧ Practice being wrong. In conflict, look for the ways in which you are responsible for the enmity. Take offense slowly and forgive swiftly.

✧ Pay attention to the rituals of repentance and renewal that you practice in your intimate relationships.

✧ How do you fight and make up, signal that you are sorry, that you forgive? With words? Gifts? Gestures?

✧ What do you do when you find out that you have been wrong and wounding?

In the end, perhaps the most down-to-earth program ever given about the practice of love is contained in the prayer attributed to Saint Francis:

O Lord, our Christ, may we have Thy mind and Thy spirit; make us instruments of Thy peace. Where there is hatred, let us sow love; where there is injury, pardon; where there is discord, union; where there is doubt, faith; where there is despair, hope; where there is darkness, light; where there is sadness, joy. O Divine Master, grant that we may not so much seek to be consoled as to console; to be understood as to understand; to be loved as to love. For it is in giving that we receive; it is in pardoning that we are pardoned; and it is in dying that we are born to eternal life.

SELF-LOVE:
Solitary Communion

Love is at first not anything that means merging, giving over, and uniting with another (for what would a union be of something unclarified and unfinished, still subordinate—?), it is a high inducement to the individual to ripen, to become something in himself, to become world, to become world for himself and for another's sake.

—RAINER MARIA RILKE

Loneliness forever and earth again! Dark brother and stern friend, immortal face of darkness and of night, with whom the half part of my life spent, and with whom I shall abide now till my death forever—what is there for me to fear as long as you are with me?

—THOMAS WOLFE

SCENE: *Dinner for One*

When she was a little girl, she had a pair of magnets, one with a black and the other with a white Scottie dog glued to the top. Her favorite game was to place them in a position of reverse polarity—nose to tail—and see how far she could get Whitey and Blackie to travel together. The trick was to keep just the right distance. If Whitey stayed too far away, there was no magnetic propulsion; if he came too close, Blackie suddenly turned around, and the positive magnetic force drew them into a face-to-face fusion, and the game ended.

Midway in her life's journey, on the rebound from a divorce after a long marriage and one of those textbook turbulent mid-life romances that are all frustrated passion, she met and began to date Mr. Almost Right. He seemed every bit an independent man with Ph.D. in hand, a ready wit, and an adventurous spirit. She was headed to Europe on an assignment for her bank, was lonely, and on a whim asked if he would like to meet her somewhere along the way. He would, and did, and they spent enchanted weeks wandering. Passing through Florence, swimming in the Adriatic, exploring the markets in Istanbul and the ruins in Athens, their conversations sparked a meteor shower of ideas, and their bodies were drawn into a common orbit of shared pleasure.

When they returned to the United States, they carried on a commuter romance between his and her cities for several months.

All was well until he decided to move to her city and stay in her apartment—just until he could find a place of his own, of course. She welcomed his visit but reminded him that she wasn't yet ready for commitment and cohabitation. Her long marriage had left her with a bad habit of ignoring her own needs and dreams, and she needed time and solitude to become acquainted with herself.

He wanted only to be with her, to blend, to marry, to be One. To her dismay, he settled into the apartment and dovetailed into her life. When she had coffee with her friends, he came along. And why not, he had no friends in her city. When her children came to visit, he joined in all the family activities. And why not, he had never married and had no children of his own. When she worked at her desk, he sat quietly in the living room and read. And why not, he had no job. The more time they spent together, the more he demanded that she agree with his judgments about her friends and family and his elaborate explanations of the dynamics of their relationship.

Within weeks the delicate distance between them that had been a playing field began to take on the character of a no-man's-land between opposing armies. She insisted they maintain separate lives. He insisted they move toward convergence. She said she needed her own space. He said she was afraid of intimacy and commitment.

As luck would have it, one day she found the very house she had been looking for near the beach and, within a week, bought it. He offered to invest his savings in the house and make an apartment for himself in the basement so he could remain near to her. She refused his offer. While she was moving her clothes from the apartment, something snapped in him. He made a series of desperate efforts to compel her to surrender, to be a couple, a family, a unit. Before her first week in her new home was over, he was phoning her ten to twenty times a day. He telegraphed her friends and children and told them she was in trouble and in need of help. He had the locks on her old (now his) apartment changed and refused to allow her to move her furniture.

On the night when he phoned repeatedly between one and four A.M. and threatened to commit suicide if she did not return, she knew she must end the relationship in order to preserve the sanity and sanctity of her own life.

In the hour before dawn she wrote the letter: "It is finally clear to me that we can't be together anymore because it would destroy both of us. You want to merge with me. You want me to surrender the integrity of my mind, experience, and judgment so we can form a single, secure unit. And you won't be satisfied with the measure of intimacy I can offer because what you want is fusion. I don't want that kind of relationship. I will not give in to the emotional blackmail of your threats of suicide. If you commit suicide, that's your choice. It would make me very sad, because I love you, but I cannot provide the meaning and center of your life. The most loving thing I can do is separate from you in a decisive way so we can both reclaim the dignity of our solitude and get on with our lives. This is good-bye. Please don't call me or try to see me. From the depth of my heart, I hope you have a good life."

The next evening she turned off her telephone, put on her favorite music, dressed elegantly, set the table with the best linen, arranged the flowers and the candles, and sat down for dinner in the solitary and luxurious company of her self.

THE IMPOSSIBLE DREAM OF FUSION

Throughout our lives our intimate relationships are shadowed by the impossible dream of fusion. Because we were formed within our mother's womb, our first experience of love was singular rather than plural. The memory of a shared bloodstream and heartbeat, of perfect communion, is encoded within every fiber of our being. Little wonder that if we are not watchful, we slip easily into an unconscious equation of love and fusion and are then dissatisfied with the limited forms of intimacy we manage to forge with our friends, spouses, and families. Measured by our earliest experience, all subsequent love relationships are inferior.

Most people will deny they desire fusion. But if you listen, you can hear echoes of the longing for the perfectly symbiotic, always harmonious love that exists only in the womb. The other day a friend who is preoccupied with the possible breakup of his marriage told me: "I have one great wish. Before I die, I would like to have a relationship with a woman in which I could tell her everything about myself, and she would accept it all. I want there to be no boundaries or barriers between us. Complete communication, understanding, and acceptance." "Oh," I replied, "you want to be completely smothered/mothered." Much that passes for love is a disguised desire to escape the burden of singularity by submerging the self in an all-encompassing relationship. The fantasy of complete merger, of two-becoming-one, both reaches backward to the womb and mimics the mystical longing to be obliterated within the secure embrace of God—"Rock of Ages, cleft for me, let me hide myself in Thee."

But we surrender to the dream of fusion without boundaries, differences, or conflicts at the cost of destroying the continual movement between solitude and communion that lies at the heart of love. Love is self-defeating when it abandons the tension between the cultivation of self and the adoration of the other.

Robust love is tidal. Sexual union is a metaphor for all profound relationships: We move from solitude toward another, lose ourselves in ecstatic union, and swim back to the island of the self. In the flow, two become one, become two, become one, become two, ad infinitum.

Love is solitary communion, being alone together. It thrives on the middle ground between the extremes of fusion and isolation. To keep it alive, we must maintain boundaries. Good fences make good neighbors.

The solitude that love requires is not to be confused with the detachment of the dance-away lover or the existentialist hero of Western culture who is forever riding off into the sunset to avoid commitment. Nor is it the self-imposed isolation of the wounded wallflower too shy to risk any deep attachments.

We cultivate solitude in order to create a hearth and home within which self-love may grow strong.

SOLITUDE AND THE SWEET BURDEN OF LONELINESS

All too often we avoid solitude and attempt to be plural without being singular because we fear the arctic wind of loneliness that blows across the most isolated reaches of the self. Whoever undertakes the journey to the interior will certainly encounter the chilling void, the terrifying fear that is adjacent to the awareness of the inevitable death that awaits each man and woman. Because we all stand alone in the presence of death and dread our ultimate abandonment, loneliness stalks our steps like a monster in the late movie. It is always just offstage waiting for an entrance. When the action slows down, it creeps in. It comes most often at unprotected times; at twilight before our bodies have shifted into the slower rhythms of the night; after waking but before we have lost the softness of sleep; in the sudden silence that calls us back to ourselves in the middle of the chatter of a party or a committee meeting. When it arrives, we usually run, get busy, keep our mind on other things. Our addiction to "love" is in large measure an effort to find an antidote to this authentic fear of ontological loneliness.

We can neither tend the solitude out of which self-love grows nor love others without s/mothering attachment until we accept loneliness as one of the seasons of life. What makes possible the light touch in love, as opposed to grasping, is the knowledge that loneliness goes with the territory. It is a sweet burden. Sometimes my loneliness seems like evidence of my personal failure—if only I were better at loving, more communal, I would not feel alone. But I look deeper, and I see that loneliness is the price of self-awareness and creativity. I must return again and again to my sanctuary to listen to still, small voices that are too hushed to be heard in the presence of any other person, to attend to the sacred and profane desires and promptings that move beneath the surface of my persona. It is only then that the face of loneliness changes, and I recognize it as the companion of love.

Self and Others: *The Heart Is an Echo Chamber*

The Golden Rule—"Do unto others as you would have them do unto you"—needs to be balanced by the Silver Rule: "Do unto your self as you would have others do unto you." Be as careful and compassionate of your self as of your neighbor. Learn to nurture, excite, and sustain your self. Discover within your self the lover who has the power to delight you.

Which comes first, gold or silver, loving our neighbor or loving our self?

One of the seldom-examined dogmas of contemporary psychology is that we must have high self-esteem before we can love others. The Golden Rule seems to have been revised to read: "First love yourself, and you will automatically love your neighbor." Certainly, if we are filled with self-loathing, we are apt to project our self-hatred onto others or demand to be loved because we are unable to love ourselves. But the ancient insight contained in the folk tale of Beauty and the Beast suggests that we may come to love ourselves by being loved by others, even and especially when we are ugly or unworthy in our own eyes. Or as the same insight was expressed in the religious tradition by Martin Luther, we may be loved by God as we remain sinners.

Fortunately, love is not a Monopoly game in which we must begin at "Go" and either proceed in an orderly way in a single direction or be sent directly to jail. There is no right and necessary place to begin the journey beyond the fortress of the ego. Those who were well loved as children and given a secure sense of self by wise parents may have a head start, but many a deprived child moves with godspeed to overcome a handicap and arrive at a heartful place. We should be careful of assuming that psychology, or any other social science, can tell us how to pick a sure winner in the race between the tortoise and the hare. Love is a wild and unpredictable quantum energy that expands in all directions and defies all the laws of linear causality. Sometimes we love out of deficiency, sometimes out of fullness. Sometimes our vacuum of self-esteem is filled by the generosity of others; sometimes exuberant self-love overflows and embraces others.

Love is a reverberatory phenomenon. Once, hiking in Canyonlands National Park, I stood at a point where three canyons converged, bellowed a song, and moments later was engulfed by an antiphonal chorus of echoes. Every human community is an echo chamber in which the effects of love (and/or hate) continuously bounce back and forth between self-other-self-other, ad infinitum.

Embracing the Multitude I Call Myself

To understand self-love, we need to put to rest some muddleheaded and superficial ideas. In authoritarian and moralistic religious denominations, self-love is frequently maligned by being identified with vanity, self-indulgence, arrogance, and unseemly pride. In popular New Age schools of psychotherapy, it is trivialized by being reduced to uncritical self-acceptance and self-applause. Those sunny-minded psycho-cheerleaders whose wares are advertised in airline magazines designed to appeal to those whose god is Success, advise us: "Create a winning self-image; program yourself for success by positive unconditional feedback; affirm yourself; practice positive thinking." This brand of pseudo–self-love substitutes a shallow self-regard for a deep, paradoxical self-acceptance and turns self-love into an uncritical autoromance, a kind of whispering of sweet nothings in one's own ear. If all I see when I look at myself is a person who is powerful, capable, lovely, beautiful, and true, you may be certain that I am looking at an airbrushed image of myself.

Authentic self-love is much more complex than self-esteem. It has nothing to do with cultivating a positive self-image and demands that we follow the difficult advice of Socrates: "Know thyself." But this prescription causes certain problems of its own. As we saw when we considered repentance, self-knowledge brings us bad news before it brings us good news. All the psycho-spiritual traditions from Hinduism to Buddhism to Freud begin with the tough observation that human beings are systematically self-deceiving. Our images of self are distorted by our need to think well of ourselves. The veil of illusion—called *maya* by the early Vedantic philosophers and the Buddha—our unconscious greed and fear, covers the eyes with which we look at ourselves. The idealized self-images that bolster our pride are, according to Marx, an ideology that serves our economic self-interest. Or in Christian language: We have all sinned and fallen short of the glory of God. We are alienated from our deepest self, our neighbor, nature, God. The illusion of niceness forces all that is dark, unattractive, excessive, crude, unacceptable, cruel to live underground, like the homeless of New York who inhabit the subway tunnels.

Begin with the awareness that you are not singular but plural. Although you call yourself by one name and refer to yourself as *a* person, you are in reality more like a loose-knit community of subpersonalities, or a cast of characters bound together by a script—your autobiography—that you are continually in the process of writing and revising.

Metaphorically speaking, each of us is a multiple personality. Ever since *The Three Faces of Eve,* psychology has been so enamored of the phenomenon of the multiple personality that it is now something of an in-joke that every therapist wants a client who is a multiple. A true multiple personality is like a failed community, in which the subselves are split off and remain in a state of disintegration and isolation with no overarching consciousness. By contrast, a "normal" person is a more or less integrated community, depending on the number of subpersonalities that are admitted into awareness and maintain some kind of mutual communication. Using this model, we can understand self-love as the process by which we gradually enfranchise all of the subpersonalities and invite them into the commonwealth of consciousness.

Here, for example, are some of the cast of characters who inhabit the stage, or lurk behind the scenes, in the private theater I call myself. Some of them I like and admire, and others I am tempted to dislike and reject.

The philosopher. Loves questions, analysis, and the intricate play of ideas. Always trying to understand *why.* Tends to think too much, gets caught in head-tripping.

The sensualist. Savors sybaritic pleasures: skin on skin, sunlight and shadows on rolling hills, strong coffee on raw February afternoons, stroking cats. Loves to look, touch, smell, taste, listen. Easily lost in the sensations of the moment.

The compassionist. Empathic, sensitive, easily moved by the plight of others, charitable. Often acts to alleviate suffering but is sometimes overwhelmed by the infinite quantity of tragedy, suffering, and evil and retreats to cultivate his garden.

The opportunist. Coldhearted, calculating, cynical. Insensitive to others' feelings. What's in it for me? What's your angle? Often uses empathy, divorced from compassion, to manipulate others. Can be charming to further his own ends.

The consumer. Insatiable. Always wants more. Stimulated by the promise of new things, experiences, people, places. Never fully satisfied. Loves flea markets, garage sales, thrift shops, mail-order catalogs, trendy stores, the latest models. Expects each new purchase, possession, relationship to fill the vacuum within.

The ascetic. Loves empty time, open space, and uncluttered existence. Lean and sparse. Simplify. Less is more. Bare bones are beautiful.

The adventurer. Loves intensity, novelty, challenge, risk, strange places, and new faces. Always moving on, pushing the frontier. A gypsy. Will try anything once. An adrenaline junkie, easily bored and intolerant of routine and abiding commitments.

The homesteader. Loves family, hearth, children, the routines and rituals of ordinary life. Grounded in place, rooted in locality. Gives and receives nurture. Faithful at heart.

The child. Wonderstruck. Looks at things with innocent eyes. Loves to play, loaf, hang out. Laughs a lot. Forgets what time it is. Has a vivid imagination, pretends, fantasizes, and plays make-believe. Ignores the rules.

Getting to know yourself is an endless study. Every year you will be disabused of many certainties, surprised to discover how little you know and how much of that is mistaken. Gradually you may become a calm observer of the many who inhabit the one who goes by your name. Studying your selves, you will become more of a true witness and more of a mystery. Do not expect in this lifetime to graduate from the university of the self.

But just because learning to love the self requires a lifetime of practice, it doesn't mean we need to surround the process with the fog of false mystification. Self-love depends on mastering the same elements that are necessary to love others. As nearly as I can tell, all the emotions, commitments, modes of care-giving, and skills that are involved in a loving relationship with my child, my wife, my friend, my neighbor, apply equally to my relationship with myself.

Additionally, loving the self requires the same kind of commitment and vows as a marriage. Promise to love and cherish all parts of your self. Have compassion for your suffering, grieve your losses, judge yourself fairly according to your best standards, repent of your failures and hardness of heart, rejoice in your good fortune, forgive your betrayals, remain faithful to your self, and nurture your potentialities now in the bud. After all, you are going to be married to yourself for better and worse, for richer and poorer, in sickness and in health, till death . . .

❧

The Practice of Solitude and Self-Love

To cultivate solitude requires a commitment of time, attention, and energy for savoring the complex relationship between me, myself, and I—the ménage-à-moi.

◇ Make this vow to yourself: "I promise I will set aside a regular time and place and create a refuge into which I will retreat to be alone with my thoughts and feelings. Within this cocoon of spacious silence, I will explore my values and my vision of the good and the best, and meditate on how I may practice the great vocation of becoming a lover."

✧ Consider how you are going to create your private retreat-center. You may want to make a special meditation room in your house, or place an altar in a corner of your bedroom. Or you may retreat into the vast silence of a cathedral at three o'clock on Friday afternoons, or to a place in the woods where the pine trees grow thick and form a secret den.

✧ If you are entangled in intimate relationships that are smothering (as most marriages, families, and friendships are from time to time), you will need to find ways to disengage sufficiently to recover your solitary center. It is always best to tell your intimates in a nonthreatening way that you need to be alone for a time. Many long-married couples find it necessary to take separate vacations or declare a sabbatical from togetherness in order to renew their solitary selves. When solitude is built into the structure of marriage and family, it becomes a wellspring for the renewal of passion. Absence makes the heart grow fonder.

✧ Listen to your desires. You are a chaotic multitude of wishes, wants, needs, appetites, urges, longings, cravings, lusts. So long as you are alive, you will be moving beyond the satisfactions of the moment, reaching out to grasp some missing X, Y, or Z. Keep asking yourself: What do I *really* want?

✧ What gifts and talents do you have that need to be nurtured in order for your boldest dream of yourself to come to fruition? What disciplines are essential for your growth? What momentary pleasures must you sacrifice to your long-term well-being?

To practice self-love, you will need to become skilled in managing the inner politics of experience and creating some kind of harmony within the diverse community of your subpersonalities. Obviously, before an inner democracy can be established, you must first give diplomatic recognition to all of your cast of inner characters and allow each to appear on the stage of consciousness.

✧ Identify and give names to the seemingly contradictory aspects of yourself—the kindly and the careless, the honorable and the dishonorable, the loved and the hated—all of the characters who inhabit you.

✧ Create inner dialogues that allow all the saints and sinners, beasts and little children, characters hiding in the shadows and ones in heavenly brilliance, a place within the commonwealth of your consciousness. The prophet may challenge the sensualist to pay more attention to justice and less to pleasure, or the adventurer may warn the homesteader that it is time to hit the open road, or the tyrant may try to curtail the spontaneity of the child (or vice versa).

✧ Monitor your inner dialogue. Sometimes I catch myself subvocalizing in destructive ways—trash talking, harshly criticizing, guilt-tripping. Eavesdrop—listen to how you talk to yourself. What tone of voice do you use? What messages do you send to yourself? Include in your self-talk all the components of loving dialogue—encourage, comfort, question, praise, laugh at, and listen to your selves.

COMMITMENT:
Willing to Love

⋙⋘

Will without love becomes manipulation. . . . Love without will becomes sentimental and experimental.

—ROLLO MAY

Love, in the fullest and most concrete sense of the word . . . seems to rest on the unconditional: I shall continue to love you no matter what happens. . . . Love, far from merely requiring the acceptance of risk, demands it. Love seems to be calling for a challenge to be tested because it is sure to emerge the conqueror.

—GABRIEL MARCEL

SCENE: *A Wedding Ceremony—Written for Friends*

Several years ago two old friends asked me to create a wedding ceremony. The bride and groom had survived a long and stormy apprenticeship and, at long last, wanted to declare their commitment to each other.

Salutation to the bride and groom:

"You are old stones, tumbled by the waves, rubbed together on the sand, long bleached in the sun; your edges have been smoothed by the abrasion and pleasure of being together. You are knowing and willing partners already bathed in the sea of common memories.

"Now you come to forge a future together that is wide enough to hold your hopes. By your promise and your continuing care for each other, you will build a house of memory strong enough to withstand the inevitable encroachments of time, pain, and tragedy.

"There is no use pretending that marriage is merely a continuation of romance, or just a ceremony that formalizes your relationship. From the moment you pledge yourselves to each other unconditionally, much will begin to change. As you make a hearth, the ancient gods and demons of childhood will return to live with you. Within the sanctuary of your intimacy, as the trust between you grows, you will finally become safe enough to allow your deepest fears of abandonment, your long-hidden shame, your impolite anger, your infantile omnipotence, your vulnerable dreams, your secret virtues, and the deepest longings of your spirit to emerge into the cleansing light of day. At long last you may drop your masks, get offstage, and explore who you are when you no longer have to pretend in order to win the love that can never be won. More than anything, marriage is the way we heal ourselves and heal each other. For it is only when we are within the arms that hold us in our brokenness and splendor that we are set free to become ourselves.

"The marriage you create will be uniquely your own. Nowhere has the story you will enact together been told before. But there is a logic that rules every love story, and you will be well provisioned for your journey if you respect it.

"Begin with the knowledge that you will often fail each other and therefore you can only keep your love alive by practicing the great art of forgiveness. A thousand times you will forget to listen, tread roughly on sacred ground, reopen each other's ancient wounds, say too much or too little, close your heart to care at the very moment compassion is needed. But your love will remain lively and green if you forgive each other a thousand and one times. And begin again.

"Remember that every day you must renew your solitude. From now on you will be going your separate ways together. Learn to be profoundly alone in each other's presence. Marriage is the sound of two hands clapping, the being apart and coming together of solitary individuals. Promise to preserve and deepen your own uniqueness, to bear the sweet burden of your freedom, to listen to the calling that life whispers only in your own ear.

"Cultivate the ground in which your common roots will now be planted. Promise to devote the time, energy, and care necessary to forge a bond of purpose and pleasure strong enough to withstand separation, periods of disillusionment, and boredom, the fires of anger and the specters of disease, old age, and death. Pursue each other's spirits and comfort each other's bodies. Be inventive in your loving.

"Finally, there is a vow that all of us who are your friends need to take together in your presence. This marriage now belongs to all of us. It is not just two people who are being joined, but two clans, two circles of friends, as well as the ghosts of former lovers. It is our responsibility to rally round to help, enjoy, and support this marriage. At times we may need to witness and offer insights only friends can give. Should you fight, and when you fall prey to the normal tragedies that shadow human life, you will need our aid and comfort. We your friends, who have loved you over long years, pledge you our care, our honesty, our troth, as you so pledge to each other."

Love, Intention, and Will

As a teenager, in the chaos and confusion of love and hormones, I asked my mother: "What is love?" "Love," she answered, "is the willed intent of the heart." In the chaos and creativity of my maturing years, I have frequently wrestled with this definition of love. Sometimes it seems love is pure grace, easy as falling, effortless as flowing. Sometimes it is hard work, hammer and tongs, the gradual forging of something of fragile beauty from steel and bronze. Love is given, *and* it must be made. To create a lifework, a marriage, a family, a friendship, a dwelling place requires de-cision, sacrifice, and compromise. And it takes determination and willpower to remain faithful to promises and commitments.

The feeling of love may blossom instantaneously or grow slowly. Sometimes it bursts into the present moment virgin-born. A newborn baby is handed to its father, and immediately a full-blown sympathy too deep for words comes into existence. A man and a woman, both battle-scarred veterans of failed marriages and romances, meet at a dinner party given by friends, fall into a conversation that continues uninterrupted for eight hours and segues smoothly within weeks into a marvelous marriage. A woman on vacation in Peru watches a homeless child begging on a street and is moved by such deep compassion that she decides on the spot to give up her comfortable life in Marin County, move to Peru, and start a home for street children. At other times, love matures over decades. Acquaintanceships gradually ripen into friendships. A couple who for years have been locked into a cycle of resentment and intimate combat make peace and enjoy harmony. Parents and children who suffered together in a troubled family grow old and learn to be kind to each other.

Regardless of whether the *sentiment* emerges suddenly or gradually, a continuing relationship between two people moves inevitably from the realm of feeling into the realm of willing. A romance that begins as an immediate attraction to a stranger across a crowded room proceeds to conversation, to caring, and possibly to cohabitation. It then escalates, inevitably, toward defining the level of commitment that will govern the relationship. Love spreads beyond the immediacy of the here and now and establishes its dominion over our future. It shapes our expectations, changes our plans, and begins to construct its empire of hope and memory.

At first, the future we plan to inhabit together may be nothing more than tomorrow afternoon. With strangers we meet on a plane or casual acquaintances toward whom we are drawn, we begin relationships with hope, caution, and short-term agreements. Getting to know one another, we remain tentative about how much we want our lives to intertwine. We agree to spend a day in the park, to go to a rodeo, concert, or baseball game. We tell each other edited versions of our life stories that reveal only what we feel is safe and appropriate.

It is well and good that the more rapidly love drives us, the more cautious we should be about commitment. A foolish heart needs the balance of a careful will. The tragedies of love are as often the result of too much commitment too early as too little commitment too late.

Traditionally, etiquette, good manners, flirting, and courtship served to cool the ardor and limit the commitment of potential lovers until they could get to know each other well enough to decide with informed hearts how much of their future they wanted to share. Most modern societies encourage people to go slowly and deliberately in developing friendships, romances, and marriages, to play and experiment with intimacy before making lasting commitments.

In the usual course of relationships, trust grows gradually out of the soil of promises made and kept. After eating bushels of bread together, one day we find we have become com-pan-ions.

The polite distance we have maintained by conscious withholding, practicing good manners, and remaining on our best behavior gives way to greater spontaneity and candor. The increasing warmth of friendship melts our reserve, and we begin to assume our relationship will endure into an unspecified future. Maybe for years or a lifetime.

Another kind of difficulty arises when long-term friendships or romantic involvements get arrested at the level of tentative commitments. "I will be your friend/lover/spouse so long as you do not ask me for money, do not make too many demands on my time, do not get fat, do not confront me about my drinking, do not criticize my business dealings, do not demand more commitment than I want to make, do not lose your sex appeal." With conditional commitment comes conditional acceptance, conditional trust, conditional openness, conditional passion, conditional security.

CONTRACTS AND LIMITED PARTNERSHIPS

But love never stands still. It must either be expanding or be declining. From immediacy and feeling it begins to spread into the domains of imagination, willing, and planning. When we feel pleasure in the presence of another person, we naturally search for ways to continue and enhance the well-being we have experienced. Likewise with compassion. If we are moved by the suffering of another, we look for ways we can change their painful present into a more felicitous future. Tending toward each other, we begin to desire, to imagine, to plan, to will, to act, to create a common future. At a certain point the stakes in the game of love are suddenly raised, and we are faced with the alternative of doubling our bet or dropping out. One person asks another: "Just what are your intentions? Where is this relationship headed?"

Many medium-cool modern hearts have been conditioned by economics, contracts, and the mentality of lawyers to be most comfortable with limited commitment. Kay Hymowitz, writing in *The Wall Street Journal* (April 6, 1995, "Where Has Our Love Gone?"), reports that we are in a postidealistic, neo-pragmatic era of relationships. Americans, she says, disdain intense emotions like grief, jealousy, and love in favor of an emotional style of smooth detachment, a profoundly rationalistic vision of human relationships that looks with suspicion on mystery, myth, and strong feelings that were once thought to accompany love. "We want pleasure and self-fulfillment but not passion. The lover—or partner . . . is in danger of becoming an object to be used and played with. The connection between partners can then only be imagined as contractual."

The problem with contractual love is that it is usually emotionally unsatisfying over the long term. In the beginning two individuals who are attracted to each other can negotiate their level of involvement, control their feelings, and give and receive measured intimacy. But willy-nilly, separate individuals who remain in intimate proximity do form entangling alliances that begin to erode their sovereignty. Two have a way of becoming one.

Metaphors taken from the realms of law and economics—contracts, negotiations, mutual rights, obligations, investments—help us understand the willful and intentional aspects of love. But to understand true commitment, we need metaphors that are taken from the organic world. In its more advanced stages, love is more like creating a fertile hybrid than agreeing to a contract. Commitment is the process by which two (or more) buds are grafted onto a common root stock.

Each pleasure shared, each promise made, each mutual plan agreed to, each common memory recalled, is a tendril we send out from our isolation that makes its way across the distance separating us and begins to graft us together. Sometime after years of disciplining our will-to-love, struggling against the temptations to cut and run, the graft begins to take, and we discover that we have grown together. Our roots have gone down into common soil, our DNA has entwined to create a new hybrid. As we settle into communion, the will-to-love gradually becomes less necessary. The oneness for which we originally had to strive has become a fact; effort is replaced by acknowledgment; autonomy gives way to interdependence.

THE AGONY OF COMMITMENT AND VOWS

When love moves beyond tentative arrangements and toward commitments and vows, we naturally become anxious.

There are questions about the right balance between spontaneous enjoyment and the necessity to "work on the relationship." Is this relationship good enough as it is, or promising enough, for me to put aside my reservations and give myself to it wholeheartedly? Or should I wait for something better to come along? Does the relationship have to be wonderful before I make a commitment, or will making the commitment transform a rocky relationship into a smooth one?

The specter of binding ourselves to cherish and care for a friend, a child, a lover, a mate, in an unknown future arouses our fears of being imprisoned within a space too small for our spirit. Every commitment is based on a decision, a choice of one alternative to the exclusion of others. Making a commitment involves self-sacrifice, voluntary self-limitation, and cutting off future possibilities. So it doesn't seem prudent to pledge fidelity without qualifications. How can I promise to maintain a relationship without risking a betrayal of myself? What if my feelings change? The risk of commitment arouses anxiety, which can be faced only with courage and the resolve to further the long-range fortunes of love.

The commitment and vows that are one element of love are not contracts that belong to the world of law but promises that can be made only in the hope that *if* we remain faithful, we may reap the full fruit of love. They are wholehearted statements of an intention to co-create a desired future, made with the realization that it takes years of common experience, shared memories, and dreams to weave the narratives of two lives into a single story and enjoy the reward of unmeasured love. Meaningful commitments come about after lovers or friends have developed deep knowledge, empathy, and care for each other. They are knowing promises, not a desperate leap in the dark.

Certainly it is risky to promise that we will continue to care for our children, our friends, our mates, to bind ourselves to conditions we cannot predict. But consider what will become of us if we do not! To cobble together a life without commitments, a life of one-night stands, tentative relationships, and limited engagements is a guarantee of superficiality and loneliness. *Entangling alliances may bind us too closely for comfort, but life without entwinement is as fragile as a rope of sand.* Without abiding commitments and vows, there are arrangements but no marriages, child care but no families, associations but no friendships, housing developments but no communities, a present but no memory of the past or hope for the future, a collection of experiences but no spirit or soul.

The pledge that we will cherish those we have chosen to love for better or worse, for slimmer or fatter, for richer or poorer, is the consequence of having accepted the love bond as something that needs fierce protection, because without it our lives would have no continuity, no depth, and no bulwark against the fickleness of circumstances.

An irrevocable promise is the precondition for wholehearted passion. I cannot act with trust and abandon until I decide that I will place the whole momentum of my being at the disposal of my decision. I become a fully engaged person only when I betroth myself, promise fidelity, to my friend, my mate, my vocation, my place, my community.

In coming to love we gradually exercise and strengthen the element of will. From desire an intention is born; from intention a promise; from promise a commitment. And perhaps from commitments faithfully fulfilled, two persons may reach a point where they desire to exchange vows to be bonded to each other.

The taking of vows lifts commitment from the private to the public, from the tentative to the absolute, from the secular to the sacred. Traditionally, marriage vows are not between two individuals but are promises made in the presence of family and community. The witnesses to vows form a third party in the relationship. That we pledge fidelity in a formal and public ceremony is a recognition that a marriage between a couple can thrive only within a context of family, friends, and community.

Traditionally, vows have been considered sacred because the pledge of unconditional love provides our only sanctuary against the ravages of time and the normal tragedies that shadow human life. I pledge that no matter what happens, I intend to remain available and caring.

And nevertheless, we often fail. The best of intentions, the most sincere of commitments, the most sacred of vows cannot foreclose the possibility that two persons will come to a fork in the road where love itself demands that they part. Sadly, early marriages and youthful friends must sometimes be left behind when they threaten to destroy the integrity of who we are becoming. Leave-taking, renouncing of vows, and divorce, although tinged with grief for what is lost and sorrow for what might have been, are sometimes necessary.

In 1971, after seventeen years of marriage, Heather Barnes Keen and Samuel McMurray Keen released each other from their vows. I do not believe they betrayed each other.

Ambivalence: *Entering Shadowland*

> *I yes when you no,*
> *rip when you sew,*
> *do when you don't,*
> *will when you won't,*
> *can when you can't,*
> *rave when you rant,*
> *wax when you wane,*
> *lose when you gain,*
> *zig when you zag,*
> *flow when you flag,*
> *yang when you yin,*
> *out when you in,*
> *And vice versa.*

We all know that "the course of true love never did run smooth" (or false love, for that matter), but we are always surprised to find that no sooner do we pledge undying love than we enter Shadowland. We thought that exchanging vows would create a private paradise of love, but once locked into "forever after," we discover the bitter Sartrean truth that "hell is other people." Many couples who have lived together prior to marriage are startled to find how radically their relationship changes the moment they marry.

Once we abandon our tentativeness and lock the door that was always kept open, the dynamics of love change. When we no longer have to be on our best behavior, when we no longer have to perform and present a pleasing persona, all that we had kept in the closet emerges. The honeymoon ends when we allow "the worst" that we have previously hidden to emerge. He finds that the shadow side of her delightful spontaneity is a careless inattention to details; she can't balance the check-book, is chronically late, and has only an occasional relationship to household order. She finds out that the shadow side of his forthright manner and sense of responsibility is a tendency to be judgmental and bossy and to try to control everything. As day after day he is confronted with disorder and she with tyranny, a new kind of ambivalence begins to infect their relationship. Both discover the no that walks hand in hand with the yes of love.

SHE: Do you love me?

HE: Yes.

SHE: Do you like me?

HE: Yes. And no.

SHE: What do you mean, no?

HE: Do you think you are always likable?

SHE: When am I not likable?

HE: Well, for instance, you don't plan very well, so you often reach a point where everything overwhelms you, you get frantic, rush around in a hysterical, disorganized way, and inject a sense of panic into the situation. If I dare to make any suggestion about a more efficient way to get things done, you start blaming me for the crisis, claim I am trying to control you, and get cold and withdrawn. I don't find you likable at times like this.

SHE: I'm not a planning type, and organization isn't my strong suit. You knew that when you married me. So now you are really confessing that you don't like who I am.

HE: No. My relationship to your relationship to time is more complex than that. If I want to stay in bed and make love in the morning, I am glad that you are not compulsive about being on time. But when you keep me waiting when you promised to meet me at three-thirty, your irresponsibility irritates me.

SHE: Why do you have to be so uptight?

HE: Does that bother you?

SHE: Of course. You would be more fun to be with if you were more spontaneous and weren't so rigid about following your plans.

HE: So you are confessing that you don't like me when I am organized and efficient.

SHE: I didn't say that. I like your efficiency when it's time to do the income tax and I haven't the foggiest idea about where the money went. But I don't like it when we are supposed to be on a vacation and you have a whole list of places we have to go and things we have to do, supposedly to have a good time.

HE: Do you love me even when you don't like me?

SHE: Yes.

HE: How do you know you love me at the times when you don't like me?

SHE: Because I still remember the good times. Because I'm willing to work at solving our problems even when it isn't fun. Because I feel we are becoming larger and better individuals because of our relationship. What about you?

HE: Even when I'm mad at you, I can't imagine my life without you.

SHE: So it is for better and for worse!

HE: In spontaneity and rigidity. . . . Do we have time to make love?

SHE: That depends on who's keeping time.

HE: Today you keep time, and I'll keep order.

SHE: Then we have plenty of time.

You will not always like the one you love. Count on it. Your beloved will have habits and characteristics that will drive you up the wall. Your adolescent children will be rude, demanding, and inconsiderate. Your friends will get fat, not bathe often enough, chew with their mouths open, drink too much, borrow money and forget to repay it.

How do we remain creatively engaged in those periods when we do not like the persona or behavior of someone we love? How do we ride out the times when we are disapproving, angry, bored, hurt, disappointed with a mate, a child, a friend?

We idealize love as a force that unites, a current of desire that draws us together. But go rafting on any wild river, and you will find that after the rapids sweep you downstream, there is always an eddy, a countercurrent, that pushes you in the opposite direction. Dynamic love involves force and counterforce, attraction and repulsion, yes and no. It is easy to celebrate the excitement of eros as it sweeps us through the white water toward the object of our desire, but much more difficult to acknowledge the counterforce that pushes us away from the one whom we also love.

Pay close attention, and you will see that there is always a tension between attraction and repulsion. The same qualities that draw me to her/him also repel me. Opposites attract (and repel). We desire and defend ourselves against the virtues we lack. Thus, as Anatole France said, lovers oscillate between the twin poles of yearning for and annoyance with.

And of course, liking and attraction may be almost totally absent from certain types of love. I may, for instance, be moved to compassion by somebody I don't like or enjoy—a troubled child, a criminal, an enemy, a person whose personality has been destroyed by disease or drugs. Doctors, nurses, and social workers regularly give tender loving care to disagreeable patients and clients. And in a different vein, as any reader of *True Confessions* knows, we may be sexually attracted to someone we neither like nor admire. The chemistry of attraction and repulsion is no less complex and strange than sexual chemistry.

In the course of a week of intimacy with my wife, my children, and my friends, I experience a kaleidoscope of emotions that range between desire and indifference, communion and isolation, contentment and dis-ease, boredom and admiration, warm communion and hot anger.

Seasoned love is not a monotone of simple liking but an emotional symphony that includes discord and ambivalence.

Unconditional Acceptance

We all long for love without measure. Or to put the matter even more strongly, we feel it is somehow our natural right, or at least our crying need, to be loved unconditionally by someone, if not everyone. In our most ego-centric moments, we think, "If only you understood me, you would love me without reservation." We secretly consider our virtues many, our vices few, and our needs justified. From within the castle of the ego, we observe that other mortals are so flawed that a prudent person must limit his or her commitment and acceptance until they have proven themselves to be lovable. Considering others' imperfections, I am naturally ambivalent, but considering my largely admirable qualities, they should love me unconditionally. In short, we demand devotion but offer only a conditional contract.

It is not uncommon to hear soon-to-be-disillusioned newlyweds confidently affirming their undying and unconditional love. But in truth there seems to be only one instance in which unconditional love commonly comes at the beginning of a relationship—with our children. In any culture that is still animated by civility and hope, the majority of parents welcome a child with open arms and boundless love. Like many parents, I knew without question from the moment my children were born that there was nothing they could ever do that would change my commitment to them. More often than not, even when the worst happens and a child grows up to be a criminal, the parents' love remains constant.

Excepting parental devotion, when it is present, unconditional love usually develops after the discovery of the flawed character of the beloved and the realization of our own ambivalence. It does not arrive *à la* Hollywood, when we finally find the perfect partner, but when we recognize with humility and compassion that I and thou are both fractions who can only be made whole by love. Romantics in search of the perfect lover are condemned to perpetual disappointment because, paradoxically, unconditional love graces only those who remain aware of their perennial imperfections. Realists know that the only option we have is to love our crooked neighbors with our crooked hearts.

Love liberates us from our somber bondage to the impossible dream of perfection and allows us to be perfectly flawed, beautifully blemished, exquisitely faulted, gnarled human beings.

Unconditional love, rare and ordinary as it is, accomplishes the only true revolution in human affairs because it alone transforms the psyche, reverses the "normal" laws of social and political behavior, and changes the social contract. What we have come to consider "the normal state of affairs" is in reality a system of human relations based on basic mistrust or civilized paranoia. The psyche and the state are both structured on a radical suspicion of others. Our psychological defense mechanisms and our military establishment have in common the working assumption that others are untrustworthy and dangerous. And indeed they often are. There is always sufficient evil in the world to make love an awe-ful risk.

It is only in the rarest cases, when a leader like Gandhi or Martin Luther King, Jr., emerges, that love becomes a working principle in politics and shifts the ground of action from mistrust to trust, from the assumption that "they" are malevolent to the assumption that "they" are like "us."

In private life, millions of ordinary individuals transform their interpersonal relationships by practicing radical trust. And then hope becomes a self-fulfilling prophecy. Act as if others are fundamentally motivated by goodwill, and you will elicit far more kindness than hostility. Assuming the risky stance of trust transforms us by a process of psychological and social disarmament. The ultimate promise of unconditional love is that when we accept and are accepted by others, we no longer need to perform in order to win love or to defend ourselves from others. If this "perfect" love, which Saint Paul claimed "casts out fear," is seldom achieved, it is nevertheless the polestar that guides our pilgrimage.

❧

The Practice of Commitment

❖ Imagine an escalating scale of commitment whose lowest level represents the kind of engagement you have with a casual business or social acquaintance and whose highest level is the vows and unconditional acceptance that exists within an ideal marriage and family. Chart the strata of your commitments. Begin with the most superficial—agreements and contracts you make with associates and acquaintances—and work your way up into the highest level.

❖ To whom and what have you committed yourself? What persons? What organizations? What work? What places?

❖ What are the unstated conditions in your intimate relationships? Fill in the blank: "I will continue to love you if _____."

✧ To whom are you committed without reservation or quali-
fication?

✧ Who is more valuable to you than your immediate happiness and self-interest? For whom would you sacrifice your time,
your health, your life?

✧ Whose promises, commitments to you, and unconditional
love have enriched your life?

✧ Enter into a conspiracy with your lover, friend, or mate to
dis-illusion yourselves in each other's presence. Allow your
warts and scars to show. Share your anger, grief, despair, fear,
self-doubt, greed. Take the risk of being seen. Advanced lovers
transform scars into beauty marks by the practice of acceptance.

CO-CREATION:
Fertility and Fruition

Lovers begin by frolicking near the shore in the shallow waters of desire, but the currents of time sweep them toward the oceanic depths where the mystery of being, freedom and creation is 10,000 fathoms deep.

—SANDOR McNAB

THE EIGHTH DAY OF CREATION

For two decades ours has been a marriage of fire and ice, a clash of opposites and a harmony of opposites. At best we complement each other; at worst we remain strangers and rivals viewing each other from different sides of the river. Periodically we edge into low-intensity conflict that flares into open warfare until we can negotiate a cease-fire, end hostilities, and let the lion and the lamb lie down together. Twice we separated with the intention to end our marriage, but we were failures at divorce and concluded that we are together for better and worse. So when a casual friend we had not seen for years asked us, "Are you two still together?" we replied, "No, we are *finally* together." It seems we have rolled a rock into our garden that neither of us can roll out.

What keeps us together? Obvious things: a rich mixture of the various elements of love; we share a child, a home, and pleasures of body and soul; and we have grown accustomed to each other's faces. But beneath surface satisfactions, our deepest bond is composed of a thousand invisible green rootlets, each the result of a small change we have undergone as a result of our interactions. Ever so gradually, we learn from each other, embrace the wisdom and passion of the familiar stranger who is both lover and teacher, and grow more capacious and kindly. Such rootlets, like the buried mycelium that undergirds a stand of seemingly independent mushrooms, keep hope alive and nurture a common love.

Over decades of practicing the difficult art of marriage, we have grown used to the cycle of the death and resurrection of passion. Just when the fire of anger threatens to reduce everything to ruins, the salamander wiggles forth from the ashes and begins a new life. Joy returns. Love remakes us.

An ongoing marriage is a crucible within which two persons are constantly being de-structured and re-created. As Wendell Berry said in the poem "The Dance":

> *For those who would not change*
> *time is infidelity.*
> *But we are married until death*
> *and are betrothed to change.*

THE MARRIAGE OF LOVE AND CREATIVITY

Love and creativity are entwined beyond the possibility of separation. Subtract creation from love, and all you have left is a hollow shell of sentimentality and a hard core of parasitic dependency. Love, in some form, can exist without one or more of the elements we have considered thus far—enchantment, desire, knowing, imagination, sensation, sympathy, and the rest—but not without creation, re-creation, and co-creation.

In fact, love and creativity have traditionally been identified as forms of enthusiasm or divine intoxication. In both cases something sacred or godlike enters, inspires, and takes possession of us. It is because of this proximity that the current of love and creation flows both ways. Love sparks creativity, but co-creativity also sparks love. That is why a lively workplace, a school, a building project, a political action caucus where people are joined in a creative effort is a much more propitious place to meet potential friends and lovers than a bar or a cruise ship.

To understand this indissoluble marriage between love and creation, let's observe a small-bang, a mini-creation—the simple and common act of making a metaphor, in this case in a poem by Ralph Hodgson:

> Time, you old gypsy man,
> Will you not stay,
> Put up your caravan
> Just for one day?
> All things I'll give you—
> Will you be my guest?
> Bells for your jennet
> Of silver, the best.
> Goldsmiths will beat you
> A great golden ring;
> Peacocks will bow to you,
> Little boys sing.
> Ah, and sweet girls
> will festoon you with May.
> Time, you old gypsy,
> Why hasten away?

Creativity and love have this in common: Each involves separate entities coming together—ideas or persons—in a way that they become something more than either was in isolation.

In Hodgson's poem an old gypsy man engages the mystery of time, giving birth to an unforgettable metaphor. Between the synapses, deep within the black hole in inner space we call the mind, there is small-bang, and a new world of meaning comes into being. And if you pay attention to the old gypsy man whose only home is the road, and remember the fleeting character of your own life, you will never again be tempted to think that "time is money."

This unnameable reality within which we live and move and have our being might itself be called a gypsy cosmos. Our one and only universe is always on the way to someplace else, moving, changing, evolving, creating and being created whence and whither we do not know. Its only stability is in evolving; its only stasis is in motion; its only being is in becoming.

Likewise, love abides in flux. If I and Thou are the same tomorrow as we are today and were yesterday, we have slipped out of the kingdom of becoming, out of the hands of the living God, out of the moving caravan of love. It is always the same time in the kingdom of love—the eighth day of creation.

LOVE'S CHILDREN

If it was just a hop and a skip from love to creation, it's barely a small jump from sex to creation.

Papa Freud taught us that anything could be a metaphor for sex. In dreams a church steeple might be a phallus in drag and a cave a cleverly disguised womb. It never seemed to occur to him that the opposite might also be true—sex might be a metaphor for something else. Creation, for instance.

Think about it. In the beginning sex is play and pleasure, and mostly in the dark. Most of the time people don't lie down together with any conscious intention to make anything beyond love. They are not intent on bonding, soul-making, actualizing the conjunction of the opposites, making an alchemical marriage between the masculine and feminine archetypes, or anything like that. They are just having a good time, wallowing in sensuality. Maybe following their bliss.

Then, quick as an orgasm, the entire arithmetic of love changes. Suddenly, Dolly and me, and baby makes three. And no matter how well we know the facts of life and the methods of contraception, no matter how much we may have longed for a child, we are astounded by the conception. Sometimes in the fullness of love a man or woman may become aware of the primal, genetic intention to create a child that is unconsciously present within their sexual desire. But regardless of whether we choose to be conscious of the intention to create that lies at the heart of sex, it remains a basic fact of nature. The bottom line is: Sexual intercourse between man and woman is plowing and planting, the sowing of seed, the surrendering of two bodies to the procreation of a child. Our deepest sexual passion is born from our drive to pass on the gift of life we have received. *Sex is an ontological drive to continue the human experiment, an urgency to create.*

But here we must be careful to separate biological fact from metaphor, literal children from virtual children. Sex may be Father Nature's way of tricking us into participating in the ongoing drama of creation, but that doesn't mean that we have to fall for the trick every time. Population pressures and the burden of raising a family in difficult circumstances being what they are, we are well advised to try to outwit Nature most of the time. But contraception should aim at preventing only the pro-creation of a child, not the co-creative activity of a couple. A loving dyad, of any mixture, lives only in the ongoing act of co-creation—creating forward or forth—making something of value that is more than the sum of the separate selves.

Love's child is both fact and symbol, the literal fruition of sexual union and a metaphor of the creativity that is an element in all true love. The gospel of love, creativity, and hope come together in the announcement: "For unto us a child is born." All forms of love ripen and prove themselves genuine by their fruitfulness in giving birth to something—*not necessarily a flesh-and-blood child*—that goes forth into the future.

RE-CREATION: *Love as Playground*

Creation is half sweat and hard work, commitment and sticking with it through thick and thin. But the other half is play and levity. To make love, the spirit of seriousness must be married to the spirit of fun.

At one and the same time, love re-creates the self and the other through delight and laughter. When I play with my child, converse with my friend, dally with my lover, the line between giving and receiving vanishes.

My friend Sol still smarts from a failed marriage and several disillusioning romances and insulates himself from further disappointment by a kind of Woody Allen–cynical, self-deprecating humor. But when he speaks about raising his daughter, his entire countenance changes. "She is the best thing that ever happened to me in my entire life. Just being with her, fixing supper, or taking her to school in the morning is a pure delight." As he talks, you can see the transformation take place before your eyes. The downward corners of his mouth turn upward into a smile, his eyes twinkle, his face softens, his voice loses its edge of sarcasm, and he becomes a new man inhabited, in spite of himself, by hope.

It's been a hard winter. I've been suffering from a mild case of the existential blues, brought on by nothing more severe than the creeping effects of age, the insult of mortality, and the tragedy of the world. My friend Jim has had real problems. Bad health and triple-bypass surgery. We get together to commiserate, as we have done regularly for the last quarter of a century. Before long we fall into the kind of mock-vicious teasing that male friends do with one another. We exaggerate our suffering, piss and moan about the world, make irreverent remarks about each other, parody our self-righteousness, turn tragic events into comedy. As we fall deeper and deeper into black humor, the pitch of hilarity gets higher and higher. One quip leads to another, until we are lost in a spiral of wisecracking nonsense, and by the time our sides are aching with laughter, each of us has been redeemed from the burden of self and re-created by the sacrament of glee.

According to Hindu mythology, the world is a manifestation of *leela*—divine play. And the Dutch historian Johan Huizinga maintained that the human species should be called *Homo ludens*—the playful animal. I suspect that whoever invented the phrase "necessity is the mother of invention" was a dull tool who had forgotten that mechanical devices were used to propel toys before they were put to work in England's "satanic mills," and that gunpowder was used for firecrackers at celebrations before it was recruited to give us more bang for the warfare buck. Love, at any rate, teaches us that pleasure is the father of creativity, and delight the mother of origination.

At the same time that love re-creates our separate selves, it creates a third entity—a relationship—that is more than the sum of its parts. Every friendship or marriage is a duplex cantilevered beyond its small foundation. Successful married couples know that together they make compromises (co-promises) and individually they make sacrifices to co-create an enduring relationship. In those terrible times when one or both persons are tempted to divorce, it is the strength of the relationship rather than the pleasure of being together that may provide the stability to weather the crisis.

Gradually, a loving relationship begins to radiate a field of energy, an ambience that creates concentric circles of conversation, belonging, support, and care and that expands beyond itself in many directions, just as individual trees planted beside each other create a forest ecology. A couple gives birth to a child, a family comes into being, two clans and networks of friends merge, and what began as a private affair begins to form a nexus that increases the level of amourdiversity.

A loving relationship is always synergistic—an action of discrete entities in which the effect is greater than the sum of the two. It often creates a shared work. Marie and Pierre Curie decipher the radioactive nature of radium. Richard Rodgers and Lorenz Hart write a hundred songs. A father, two sons, and a daughter form a family trapeze act and their midair choreography is so graceful, intricate, and precise that they move as a single entity. A ghetto family organizes other families to drive drug dealers out of their neighborhood. In the arithmetic of love, one plus one always adds up to more than two.

CREATIVE FIDELITY: *The Test of Love*

Understanding the link between love and creativity sheds some light on one of the most agonizing questions lovers face. Most intimate relationships reach plateaus—times of staleness, swamps of despond—when it seems hopeless or destructive to continue. When should we stop trying and call it quits? Say good-bye? End a friendship? Renounce our vows? Get a divorce? Disown our difficult family?

Love may die and not rise again. Or what appears to be fidelity may be betrayal of self and others. In the name of love many people remain in disastrous alliances, maintain abusive marriages and destructive families. When does faithfulness become a vice?

Clearly, the strength of an intimate connection is no measure of its health or creativity. The bonds we forge may liberate or imprison us, destroy or re-create us. Fatally attracted, epoxy-bonded, star-crossed lovers from Romeo and Juliet to Bonnie and Clyde have fallen into a form of mutual possession that resembles a fanatical minicult. Gang membership confers a strong sense of belonging that destroys the fragile integrity of its members. So do alcoholic families.

Gabriel Marcel is one of the few philosophers who have explored the link between creativity and fidelity. It would be disastrous, he says, to identify fidelity with mere constancy or tenacity in fulfilling the letter of the promises one has made. Fidelity, far from being a kind of inertia, involves an active and continuous struggle against the sclerosis of habit.

When a relationship has become moribund, it is a travesty to remain faithful merely because of an obligation or a promise that was once given in good faith. We often betray both ourselves and others by holding on to commitments long after they have ceased to be creative, out of inertia, fear of the unknown, and the habit of resentment. A marriage or friendship can disintegrate into a shared addiction, a bad habit that no one has the courage to break.

Destructive fidelity produces a contracting relationship of fearful and hostile dependency, within which withholding, competition, resentment, retaliation, and alienation grow more powerful each year and spread beyond the dyad to infect family and friends. Perhaps the best name for such parasitic relationships is *destructive coherence*. (The popular term *co-dependence* is confusing because healthy intimacy always involves a vital form of interdependence.)

The test of whether we should call a relationship love is whether it is re-creative and co-creative. Creative fidelity produces an expansive relationship within which the practice of all of the elements of love we have considered grows more powerful each year and spreads beyond the dyad to generate a community of care, embracing family, friends, and strangers.

∾✕∾

THE PRACTICE OF CO-CREATIVE LOVE

✧ To get a rough measure of whether your love relationships are creative or destructive, whether the *eros* that binds you to others is heavenly or demonic, consider which are centrifugal and which are centripetal. Which spin you out into larger circles, and which pull you into ever smaller circles?

✧ With whom do you feel large, expansive, bold, energetic, inventive, generous, in touch with your own gifts and creative vocation?

✧ With whom do you feel small, fearful, resentful, defensive, possessive, constricted, ashamed, cut off from your own gifts and creativity?

✧ If your lovemaking has led to the pro-creation of a child, how faithfully and inventively have you nurtured and tended your co-creation?

✧ Which of your intimate relationships are mutually re-creational and renewing? Which are depleting?

✧ With whom do you co-create metaphorical children?

ADORATION:
Wondering Love

〜✕〜

Believe me, if all those endearing young charms
Which I gaze on so fondly today,
Were to change by tomorrow and fleet in my arms,
Like fairy gifts fading away,
Thou would'st still be adored as this moment thou art,
Let thy loveliness fade as it will,
And around the dear ruin each wish of my heart,
Would entwine itself verdantly still.

—THOMAS MOORE

SCENE: *The Inalienable Right to Adoration*

Several years ago a woman spoke with me about her depression and lack of self-esteem. "My problem," she explained in a highly agitated tone, "is that I come from a dysfunctional family."

"I dislike that cliché," I said. "Machines function or don't. People love, hate, hope, despair, hurt, hit, hug, laugh, cry, destroy, create, and do and feel a million other things. But they don't 'function.' Please use another word to tell me what you mean."

"I was never adored," she said.

"Were you beaten, or verbally or sexually abused, or ignored?" I asked.

"No. As a matter of fact, I was rewarded and praised when I kept my room clean, got good grades, and went with the 'right' boys. And now my parents even respect me because I am successful and make a lot of money. But they never adored me. And neither did my husband."

"Do you think you should be adored?" I asked.

"Yes."

"So do I," I replied, without hesitation.

RESPECT: *Love at Second Sight*

I have often reflected on this conversation. What did she mean? What did I mean? I am sure my instinctive reply was on the mark, but I don't yet understand why. Clearly, my unhesitating affirmation was based on an assumption that she, like everyone, has a God-given, inalienable right to be adored.

I am struck by how much we all secretly want to be adored and by how ashamed we seem to be of this desire. Psychologists are quick to attribute this wish to an infantile fantasy of being the center of everything, but I think they confuse adoration with idolization. Our basic desire is not to be placed on a pedestal but to be recognized as worthy of attention and love.

The notion of adoration is a tangled ball of twine that will lead us into the heart of the mystery of love if we untangle it. To do this we need to look at two members of the same family of words—*respect* and *admire*.

In common usage *respect* belongs to the cool rather than hot part of the spectrum of love, nearer to admiration than to passionate desire. It suggests the recognition of worth based on good character and achievements. Albert Schweitzer, Nelson Mandela, Gloria Steinem, or Georgia O'Keeffe earned our respect because they consistently acted in ways that were creative, honorable, courageous, and wise. In short, common usage reflects the questionable idea that respect must be earned and love must be deserved.

We get nearer the link between adoration and respect if we trace the root of respect into the deeper soil from which it gets its meaning. The literal meaning of *respect* is "to look back and regard with consideration." If we think of romance as love at first sight, then respect is the kind of love that develops with second sight, third sight, fourth sight, ad infinitum. Hidden within the meaning of *respect* is an implicit recognition that there is a profound difference between first and second sight.

Because we are all products of our childhood, we come to new experience with a long history of hopes and disappointments. Inevitably, our first sight is governed largely by unconscious prejudices, preconceptions, and categories that filter our awareness and allow us to place the unknown into familiar pigeonholes. Initially, we see others through a screen, or template, that sorts them into a simple set of survival-based categories: desirable or fearful, promising or threatening, attractive or unattractive, interesting or not interesting. The first time we see a stranger, what we see is largely a reflection of our own hopes and fears.

If you think back over the history of the people you have loved and hated, you will discover that many times your first impressions were so totally wrong, your judgments so inaccurate, that in retrospect you wonder how you could have been so mistaken. Love teaches us to look again and again, not be satisfied with what we see at first glance.

If I look at you again and again, I will soon discover that you keep eluding me, escaping my categories, transcending my understanding. You turn out to be different from what I prejudged and imagined, hoped or feared. You are not a graspable thing, not an "it" that I can sum up, possess, or control. Each time I think I have you pinned down, you change, become something different from my icon of you. You are an autonomous center of freedom, power, and desire over which I have no control, and this means that I can enter into relationship with you only as one free person with another free person.

Recognizing your freedom, I am obliged to refrain from invading you against your will, using you for my own ends, or laying siege to your inner sanctum into which I have not been invited. (Lovers obey "no trespassing" signs.)

With respect comes the disillusionment of the romantic hope of "two hearts beating as one" and the realization that in love we remain joined to a familiar stranger. No amount of knowledge or feeling of unity dispels the essential mysteriousness of the other. For all our talk about bonds, ties that bind, complete understanding, and total communication, there remains an ineradicable strangeness and separateness in love. The more deeply we re-spect, the more we recognize that those we love most will always remain free, full of surprises, inexhaustibly mysterious.

ADMIRATION AND LOVEWORTHINESS

At first glance *admiration,* the second member of our family of words, suggests that love is based on the recognition and valuing of achievements. In a capitalistic culture, where work, performance, and reward go together, it is natural (but wrong) to assume that love should be bestowed on us as a result of what we have accomplished.

The root meaning and definition of *admire,* however, points us in a very different direction. *Admire*: "from *ad + mirari* to wonder, to regard with wonder or astonishment, to regard with wondering esteem accompanied by pleasure and delight." Notice that there is nothing in the primal or root meaning of *admiration* that suggests moral achievement, excellent accomplishments, or well-deserved honors. To admire is to be astonished and delighted with the existence of an other.

Two readers of the semifinal version of this book objected strenuously to divorcing love from accomplishments and achievements. But I hold to this point because it is crucial to understand that, first and foremost, love is the state of wonder at the mere existence of another. It need not be earned. It is not a reward for a moral or productive life. It is not a recognition that someone has been a good scout—trustworthy, loyal, helpful, friendly, courteous, kind, obedient, cheerful, thrifty, brave, clean, and reverent.

If I had to choose the single best starting point for thinking about the complex nature of love, it would not be the passionate embrace of two lovers but the moment a father and mother first look with astonishment at their newborn child. In the beginning we are loved simply because we have emerged from the fertile void to begin the long human journey. No matter how many elements we may add to the compound of love, we must return time and again to this ontological astonishment.

> *Kneeling before every manger,*
> *every miracle of existence,*
> *love is born in wonder*
> *and never outgrows*
> *its swaddling clothes.*

Nothing short of the realization that we are loveworthy because we exist allows us to understand that most radical and redemptive type of love that early Christians named *agape*.

Agape, as opposed to *eros*, is the capacity to love "worthless" people, those who are not comely, morally attractive, or desirable in any way—a murderer, a ne'er-do-well who has frittered away a life. The assumption that undergirds *agape* is that at the deepest level love is based not on desire but on the astonishing fact that human beings exist. You exist; therefore you are loveworthy.

This is the sense of the famous plea in Arthur Miller's play *Death of a Salesman:* "I don't say he's a great man. Willy Loman never made a lot of money. His name was never in the paper. He's not the finest character that ever lived. But he's a human being, and a terrible thing is happening to him. So attention must be paid. He's not to be allowed to fall into his grave like an old dog. Attention, attention must be finally paid to such a person."

So adoration comes around again to the first element of love—attention—and shows us how the practice of love, without the benefit of dogma or theology, brings us into the vicinity of the sacred. In Buddhist cultures the recognition that every human being has an inalienable right to adoration is expressed in the daily ritual of greeting. Strangers and friends meeting on the street place their hands together in a prayerful gesture, bow to one another, and say *"Namaste"*—the god within me salutes the god within you. Thus they express reverence for the intrinsic sacredness of each life.

❧

THE PRACTICE OF ADORING

According to Plato and Aristotle, philosophy begins with wonder. Love, likewise. To be either a philosopher or a lover, it is necessary to recover the innocent eye of childhood, to culti-vate the habit of re-specting, so that we may see things and people freshly.

✧ Pick a person you find unattractive, undesirable, or mor-ally inferior, someone with whom you do not want to be in any intimate relationship. In your imagination try to strip away all of the characteristics that make him or her undesirable until you are left with nothing but the astounding fact that this human being has emerged from the void and exists for a brief lifetime. Notice what happens to your feelings as you make this thought experiment.

✧ Now, pick a familiar love—a spouse, a friend, a child, a parent. Notice how you habitually understand and describe this person. Notice the characteristics you love—or that have be-come slightly boring. Just for fun, throw away your entire in-ventory of categories and cease to "understand" this familiar person. Stop explaining. Stop expecting. Stop knowing. Imag-ine you are seeing your boyfriend, wife, father, child, for the first time. Notice what happens to your feelings as you make this thought experiment.

✧ If your mate or lover has had, or has been tempted to have, an affair, look at your partner through the eyes of the other woman or the other man. The other woman or the other man saw and appreciated something that you failed to see and appreciate. An affair is an X ray of longing, a diagno-sis of what has been ignored, a signal of where to find the stranger in your familiar partner. Allow your beloved to escape from the procrustean bed of familiarity, and you will dis-cover an untamed and wonder-ful person waiting to meet you at the edge of the forest. And you never can tell what will happen next.

✧ Create your own overt or hidden gesture of blessing to acknowledge the infinite worth of lovers, friends, and strangers with whom you come into daily contact. It may be a smile, a caress with the eyes, a brief touch, a special greeting.

SEXUALITY:
Carnal Love

❧

It's a funny thing, to feel one's passion—sex desire—no longer a sort of wandering thing, but steady, and calm. I think, when one loves, one's very sex passion becomes calm, a steady sort of force, instead of a storm. Passion, that nearly drives one mad, is far from love.

—FRIEDA LAWRENCE TO D. H. LAWRENCE

SCENE: *Sacrament of Flesh and Matter*

Between lovers, sex is not a thing apart but a part of whatever is happening. Like a chameleon, it takes on the color of its environment. Depending on the day and the mood, it is serious or whimsical, titillating or soulful, passionate or matter-of-fact, angry or tender, abusive or nurturing. Every time there is a major alteration in one or both partners—an identity crisis, a life-threatening illness, a shift of values and goals—the sexual dimension undergoes a corresponding change.

A few weeks ago we found ourselves in the middle of an emotional earthquake in which long-buried resentments and secret truths surfaced. Days later the tectonic plates of our beings shifted and unleashed new sexual energies.

This morning she wakes at four A.M., restless. Later today she is leaving on a ten-day trip, and she already has the road on her mind. I stir, roll toward her, and we begin making love in the heavy darkness. Still half-asleep, trailing dreams, we have not yet put on our personalities or daytime faces. Our bodies seem to be indistinct forces, impersonal, moving together like incoming waves from the ocean meeting outgoing waves of an inlet. A storm at sea tosses us together into a powerful liquid swirl. Afterward there is perfect calm, and we drift back toward sleep.

Just before I disappear through the veil of consciousness, for some reason beyond reason the old definition of a sacrament swims to the surface of my mind—"an outward and visible sign of an inward and invisible grace." Feeling the small wavelets of pleasure still washing through me and the warm entwined limbs of my wife, I imagine that our bodies, like the world into which we will soon awaken, are composed of numberless multitudes of beings interacting in a Dionysian love ritual. The whirling molecules in my mind, the pulsations in my loins, and the early morning caws of crows and twittering of flycatchers are all part of an erotic dance. We are together in this conspiracy, this sweet breathing-together, this making of love.

SUNDERED SEX AND WHOLESOME LOVE

If you have read this far (and not just flipped to this section on sex in hope of a quick fix), you no doubt have noticed that wherever possible I have systematically delayed any consideration of the sexual aspect of love. There is method in this madness.

We get to the essence of sex faster by starting with love than we get to the essence of love by starting with sex.

If we start down the narrow and tangled path of sexual intimacy in our quest for love, it is very difficult to get back on the broad path that leads to care, commitment, compassion, and community. But if we consider the other elements of love first, we can more easily understand the nature of wholesome sexual love.

Once we recognize that wholesome sexuality is an expression and celebration of wholesome love, there is not much left to say.

Sex, sexual knowledge, and sexual technique become special categories only when they have been divorced from the soulful, relational, familial, and communal contexts that distinguish human sexuality from animal rutting. What we have labeled "sex" in the modern world, and obsessively promoted in the media, is a symptom of alienation, disintegration, and desecration. Sex apart from love is a vain and destructive effort to separate sensation from feeling, passion from compassion, body from spirit, present pleasure from memory and hope. The fortunes of love rise in direct proportion to the decline of "sex" as a separate category of our thinking and living.

The best single way to heal our troubled, schizophrenic approach to sexuality would be to adapt the Balinese saying "We have no art. We do everything as beautifully as we can." Thus: "We have no 'sex.' We do everything as lovingly as we can."

There is no sexual technique, practice, or wisdom to be learned other than what is involved in mastering the other aspects of love. The best way to become a good sexual partner is to concentrate on becoming a loving human being. Practice paying attention, listening, empathy, compassion, sensuality. Nothing more, nothing less.

At worst, our reigning sexperts tempt us to employ techniques to make us more comfortable in intimate situations where sex has been reduced to an interaction between two bodies designed to produce the maximum sensation. At best, our "how to do it" manuals and videos stimulate our imaginations, assure us that we are "normal," and give us permission to experiment.

Sexual love is a way of being together. It is not having (mutual possession) or doing (exercising skills) but being present and vulnerable in the fullness of our being.

Without question, anonymous sex can be very exciting. The appeal of the strange, the unknown, the dangerous, arouses, frightens, and tantalizes us. It triggers our infantile fantasy of pleasure without responsibility, ecstasy without consequence. But like any drug that stimulates our nervous system, anonymous sex may become an addictive narcotic that destroys the delicate connection between body and soul. There are expert sexual performers— men and women who have honed a repertoire they can apply to any partner in a casual encounter, or in a pornographic performance—but the result is sex without self-revelation, awe, or spiritual vulnerability. By contrast, whole-hearted sexual lovers remain amateurs, for whom sexual touch is wonder-ful and alluring. In full bodied-and-spirited love, shyness may be an adornment, a respecting of the delicacy of the tendrils we extend when we open and touch each other deeply.

OUR GNARLED SEXUALITY

If we define ourselves, as I have insisted, as biomythic animals, then we demolish all sexual orthodoxy, all sexual stereotyping, all "one size fits all" systems of sexual technology. If our biochemistry, bodies, and minds are inseparable from the songs and stories that give dramatic structure to our experience, it is only reasonable to assume that our libidos are likewise informed by our personal and communal myths.

Consider the variety of personal myths and patterns of sexual desire that are revealed in any newspaper that prints "personals." For instance:

Quiet boy, 19, digs music, movies, coffee, Star Trek, and sweet cuddly stuff. Seeks nice girl to spend time with and share uncomfortable silences.

Englishman, bachelor, Bob Hoskins type, mean but lovable. Wants a bossy, skinny, leggy, mouthy, brainy black girl to be his sweetheart.

Men's social group seeking other men who desire to share a common interest in wearing women's lingerie and meeting other men for support.

Bisexual male transvestite seeking bisexual female (prefer size 12).

Handsome European guy seeks his American dream, 2 bi females for discreet fantasy fulfillment.

Let's watch movies on your big screen TV or cruise our bikes downtown. I'm looking for a guy with sexy scars to shower with flowers. I'm 21, SWF.

6', 175 lbs, attractive guy in search of personal growth and some fun, too. Seeks confident, sultry female to meet in public spots and share verbal fantasies.

Butch desired, 5'7, athletic, educated, sensitive heart, spiritually inquisitive, 40 yrs+, no smoking or drugs.

Traditionally, in polite Western society, such sexual variations were judged to be "perverse." But while the moralism implicit in the idea of perversion has softened, the spate of books that present the (supposedly) standard variations of sexual positions and techniques of arousal bear silent witness to the persistence of the notion that there is a single "normal" sexuality. And I venture to guess that a majority of those who buy such books suffer from an unspoken fear that they do not measure up to the norm.

An empathic and compassionate reading of sexual want ads suggests that sexual desire is as idiosyncratic and individual as fingerprints. No biological explanation will allow us to understand "Bisexual male transvestite seeking bisexual female (prefer size 12)." Only a complete autobiography provides the story that makes sense of any individual's sexual preferences. Each of us is twisted, molded, and informed by unique life experiences and thus aroused by a very narrow range of possible sexual stimuli. To be attracted only to those who resemble the "sexy" icons of popular culture, the officially beautiful playgirls and handsome playboys, is itself a kind of perversion.

There is no standard human sexual story. We are all gnarled.

Nowhere is the essence of who we are so distorted by illusion, confusion, bad faith, and blind compulsion as in our sense of gender and sexuality. Long before we reach the age when we have sufficient self-awareness to choose our responses to other people, we are unconsciously programmed by cultural software—myths, roles, expectations, gender stereotypes—that inform our experience of self and others. Men learn that, to qualify for the honorific "masculine," they must be rough, tough, hard to bluff, sexually omni-potent, and ever-ready. Women are conditioned to hone their "femininity" by being sugar, spice, and everything nice—that is, not too threatening, aggressive, or demanding.

Our notions and feelings of what is sexually desirable are superimposed over our natural desires in the same way that our desire for brand names—Calvin Klein or Giorgio Armani—is superimposed over our primal need for clothing. As a result, sex gets permeated by impulses to conquer, to control, to perform, in order to win approval and love and tranquilize feelings of loneliness and insignificance. Between the image and the reality falls the shadow. Macha and macho, like tires that have sprung a leak, must be constantly pumped up, else they become flat.

❧

THE PRACTICE OF LOVING SEXUALITY

As far as I have been able to discover from several decades of experience and observation that should not be called "research," there are only a few disciplines relevant to developing a practice of loving sexuality.

❖ Follow the Zen maxim that advises: "Don't just do something, sit there." Begin by un-doing, dis-illusioning, de-structuring, de-mything the stereotypes of "masculine" and "feminine." Throw away the labels, break down the pigeon-holes.

❖ An ancient Zen koan posed the paradoxical question: "What was your face like before you were born?" Who were you before you were defined as a man or a woman, heterosexual, homosexual, or bisexual? What was the shape of your sexual desire before you were taught to act in a "manly" or "womanly" way?

❖ Ever so delicately, tease apart your sexual presentation from your sexual essence, your mask and your substance, the stylized "masculine" or "feminine" body you present to the world and the body of desires that comes out to play in your private fantasies and dreams.

✧ Move away from false pride, from the effort to be "sexy," and sink into the proud earthiness, the fundamental humility, of your unique body.

Since the practice of loving sexuality is a duet, it depends on creating a harmonious relationship between passion and compassion, the desires of the self and those of another. To create a wholesome sexuality, to separate the wise from the foolish, the creative from the destructive, the superficial from the profound, the kindly from the abusive, practice all the elements of love.

✧ Commit yourself to the lifelong art of becoming a lover. Cultivate a compassionate heart and a passionate enjoyment of the neighbor, the mate, the family, the friends, and the mystery of this world you are graced to touch for such a brief and precious moment in time.

ENCHANTMENT:
Disillusionment and Renewal

In my end is my beginning.
—MARY, QUEEN OF SCOTS

In my beginning is my end.
—T. S. ELIOT

SCENE: *Once upon an Enchanted Time*

An instant ago, in the spring of 1950, Dover, Delaware, was redolent with the scent of lilacs, and I was nineteen and in love and filled with promise. Every little breeze seemed to whisper "Louise." Birds in the trees whispered "Louise." And Louise was all mine, and I was hers—completely and forever. In that long-ago-and-far-away zone of enchantment, time and space were different from ordinary time and space. Time was divided between the pedestrian hours I spent studying, going to class, doing laundry, and the like, and the eternal moments when we walked by the lake holding hands or sat in the parlor and kissed (when the dean of women wasn't looking). For endless hours we talked about our relationship, weaving together the story of our future, and inflaming each other with the imagined delights of our coming marriage. Space was likewise divided between the empty and the full. When I entered the dining hall, I could tell immediately whether it was a void filled with a hundred students having breakfast or a pleroma suffused with the presence of Louise. There was no cliché of young love that we did not experience as absolute truth. We knew beyond the shadow of a doubt that our love was evidence of the providence of God and that we were bound for bliss. We swam into the depths of each other's eyes, drowned and returned to life regularly. Every morning when we met and touched, the world began again. After a day at the beach where we lay quietly looking into the fire, I wrote in my diary, "This has been the happiest day of my life."

With summer we separated, she to her home and I to the wilds of Pennsylvania to work on pipeline construction. With overtime, at time and a half, my days stretched from dawn to dark, leaving me with energy enough for nothing but my daily letters to and from my beloved. Midsummer I went to visit her and regained paradise for a weekend. But fall found us in different colleges smooching by mail and vowing endless love.

In April, the cruelest month, she came for the spring dance, and after the last waltz, sudden as death, she told me she didn't love me anymore.

The final day I spent with her, I was in shock trying to make my way through the wreckage of my castle of meaning. Her every endearing feature—her eyes, her smile, the way she combed her hair—was an icicle stabbing deep into my body. When she left, I collapsed into grief and incomprehension. Why? Why? Why? I never heard from her again. No letter. No calls. No explanations.

The months that followed my exile from the Garden of Innocent Love were a parable of fallen time. No matter where I looked, Louise wasn't there. All meaning, delight, and promise seemed to have vanished from my life. Disillusioned, I plodded heavily from day to day toward nothing luxurious, unaware that I would someday find my way again into the zone of enchantment and recover innocence and hope.

Twice upon a Time: *Disillusionment and Reenchantment*

In the disappointment and disillusionment that follow our first fall into and out of love, the three most common responses are pessimism, romanticism, and realism. Pessimists decide that love is an illusion and protect themselves against further disappointment by avoiding intimacy. Romantics make a habit of falling in love but cut and run when the going gets tough. Realists decide to abstain from the excesses of romance and settle for practical, "mature" (slightly gray) relationships. Each of these responses retards growth into the fullness of love.

In the vast repertoire of world mythologies, the theme of paradise lost and regained—innocence, disillusionment, renewal—occurs again and again. In the Judeo-Christian drama, history is a three-act play: Act I—The Garden of Eden; Act II—The Fall into Alienation; Act III—The Coming of the Kingdom of God. The Zen story of the evolution of human consciousness tells a similar tale. In the beginning a mountain was a mountain and a tree was a tree; when I began to study, a mountain was no longer a mountain and a tree was no longer a tree; when I became enlightened, a mountain was again a mountain and a tree was again a tree.

This theme of innocence lost and regained is as central to the experience of love as to enlightenment.

We can never recapture the full magic of first love. And as Stephen Vincent Benét said, "Only a fool goes searching after the wind that blew across his heartstrings yesterday." Nevertheless, we may reenter the zone of enchantment again and again. In fact, each time we love in any way, we discover that our self-image and worldview undergo a radical change. The rigid structures of our personality, our limited sense of what is possible, our defense mechanisms, our habit of competition and one-upmanship are transformed. It is as if there is a chemical element in love that dissolves our hardness of heart, an elixir that reverses our spiritual arteriosclerosis. Touched by love, the self dilates, stretches, expands, and we find ourselves living at the center of an *incalculable* reality. Because we can never predict what we may become when we surrender to the imperative to love, our minds are no longer bound by the alternative of optimism or pessimism.

Without benefit of moonlight and roses, raging hormones or hyperbole, the experience of seasoned love re-creates in us a second innocence, a freedom from cynicism or guile, an openness to marvel. It is when we enter the zone of enchantment for the second time that we discover that love has the power to dispel despair and open us to hope.

When Jesus and other spirit-intoxicated men and women testify that "unless you become as little children you cannot enter the Kingdom of Heaven," they are not advising us to remain perpetual romantics, youthful Peter Pans, dance-away lovers, the *puer aeternus* and *puella aeterna* of Jungian psychology. They are making a much more radical suggestion: that abiding love in any of its manifestations repristinizes, renews, and restores us to our original condition of purity, to the spiritual and cosmic order we inhabited before the Fall.

In the degree that we live outside the charmed circle of love, our feet remain on solid ground. We exist within the "normal" reality as it is reported by the *Times*, the *Sentinel*, the *Chronicle*. The horizon of our existence is the same cycle of ego-trips, wars, and power struggles that are old as history and predictable as self-interest and death. The law of cause and effect governs everything. Nothing really new ever happens, and what counts as wisdom is the usual cynical group of clichés. The sun rises, and the sun sets. Empires rise and fall. The race is to the fleet, and the battle to the strong. Money makes the world go 'round. God is on the side of the big guns. Politics is a win-lose game. To the victor belong the spoils. And love is only a social contract, a measured compromise by which mutual needs are satisfied.

And then it happens. Falling, falling, falling. The ground beneath your feet opens, and you plunge down the rabbit hole into a topsy-turvy world where the old rules no longer apply. In the zone of enchantment everything is governed by what might be called metaphysical generosity.

Suddenly, or gradually, you begin to love a sweetheart, a mate, a child, a grandchild, a friend, a parent, *inordinately*. Your beloved, rather than your ego, becomes the center of your concern. You stop calculating and measuring your affection and give without counting the cost. You don't bargain or withhold. You surrender, stop playing power-games, cease trying to control. Your greatest delight becomes the giving of delight.

When you love, you cease to be an anonymous person in a haphazard world and feel yourself privileged, chosen, honored by love. And the new world is charged with meaning: "Every little movement has a meaning all its own." It is almost as if the one you love is an emissary from a kinder and more graceful order of reality—what we once called "an angel." In the presence of your loved one, your heart beats a little faster; you feel a little dizzy. And unaccountably, you are shy.

The other day I was visiting my son, my daughter-in-law, and my first granddaughter, when two of my son's male friends and their wives came calling with babies in tow. The mothers saw their opportunity for a respite and took off for the hills, leaving behind three babies, all under a year in age. After the usual manly rituals of worktalk and sportspeak, the men fell into conversation about pregnancy, birth, and child care. With glowing faces they talked about how fatherhood had changed their lives, how surprised they were by the daily joy of holding, tending, and playing with their newborns. Like teenage lovers they built castles in midair, planning the delights into which they intended to initiate their children—walks in the hills, camping trips, mountain-biking expeditions, and so on. Observing these young men, two of whom I had tended through the ecstasy and agony of adolescent love, I witnessed the return of innocence and enchantment on an ordinary Sunday afternoon.

No matter when and between whom it happens, love is always for the first time. A son visits a father whom he has scarcely known and from whom he has been alienated. After years of silence they begin to speak of their loneliness and longing, and for the first time they fall in love with each other. And everything is new. Two disillusioned veterans of combat in the erogenous zones circle around each other, wary as wounded animals, until one day they discover that somehow, against all odds, they have come to trust and love each other. And their world begins again.

"As it was in the beginning, is now, and evermore shall be." When we love, we live in a reenchanted world that is governed more by what may yet happen than by what has already happened, by possibilities that lie beyond our wildest imagination. Because the most common garden variety of daily love shatters our illusion that we understand the limits of the possible, it puts an end to ordinary history. Within the horizon we inhabit when we love, we do not know what we may yet become. Therefore, love is inseparable from hope. It is in this sense that we may understand Gabriel Marcel's statement in *Homo Viator*: "It is not possible to sit in judgment on the case of hope without at the same time trying the case of love."

III

❧

MEDITATION ON FAITH, HOPE, AND LOVE

LOVE AND
THE COMMONWEALTH
OF BEING

Love is an arrow shot from the bow of longing that flies out of
sight into the great Beyond.

—SANDOR MCNAB

Wherever there are two, they are not without God; and wherever
there is one alone, I say I am with him. Raise the stone, and there
thou shalt find me; cleave the wood, and there am I.

—THE OXYRHYNCHUS PAPYRUS

LOVE: A DEFINITION

What is love?
The eros uniting atom to atom to Adam and Eve,
the desire moving us to couple and create,
the promise drawing many into One,
the oak waking from its long sleep in the acorn,
the moon and womb waxing and waning,
the tide and phallus rising and falling,
No-man's land. Or woman's.
Every body's home.
Meet me there.

The time is ripe to return to the starting point of our journey to the question of love and the meaning of life. We need to explore the ancient and perennial hope that the interpersonal love that joins us to our dearest ones is of the same substance as the energy that informs our personal origin and destination and the mind-force that is continually creating the cosmos.

The grandaddy of all the existential questions that haunt human beings has been stated in many ways. Is there a benevolent intent in the cosmic drama? Is care rather than carelessness the underlying matrix of Being? Does the Creator love His/Her creation? Is there any moral direction in the nonhuman universe?

Religion in its many forms is an elaborate cultural enterprise that rests on a leap of faith that transforms our soulful questions, shy promises, and hesitant hopes into affirmations about Reality. To the existential question "Is the universe ultimately care-ful?" it answers: God is love, Allah is merciful, the world is a manifestation of the compassionate Buddha, or (in the more philosophical language of Hegel) Being-Becoming-Itself is Love or Spirit disporting with itself.

It is easy to get lost in the lush symbolism and interesting differences of the world's great religious traditions, but this should not obscure the essence of the vision that is common to all. If we strip away the liturgies, the ecclesiastical pomp and claims to authority, the moralistic codes and the dogmatic pronouncements that clothe each historical religious tradition, we find the core religious impulse is an affirmation: Love is both the pathway to and the revelation of what is most real.

To understand the religious claim, it may be helpful to differentiate it from some of the usual assertions made about love. Love may be a beautiful feeling; it may make us happy; it may be the highest achievement of a mature psyche; it may forge strong social bonds. But none of this touches the daring religious assertion that love reveals the ultimate truth about reality. Beyond the psychological and sociological levels, love is an awareness of the nature of Being. It is cognitive, a perception of what is true, not a feeling about something we wish, will, or desire. As Gabriel Marcel stated the matter, "Love is the essential ontological datum" that provides us a concrete approach to the mystery of Being. In the words of the Gospel of John: "Those who love know God."

What is being claimed here is so radical, it is easy to miss. The scientific method claims that the only way to discover the hidden truth about reality is to assume the perspective of an objective, dispassionate observer. The religious method claims that the only way to discover the hidden truth about reality is to become a passionate and compassionate participant. Love is both a path and a destination, a way of knowing and the "object" that is known.

It is from within the experience of love that the great religious-spiritual visions of humankind have emerged. And from the religious perspective, love is inseparable from faith and hope. Indeed, all are different aspects of the same intuition about the ultimate human destiny. Love is the third eye that in-visions the unity of Being beyond the obvious plurality. It is the third ear that detects the hidden harmony within the cacophony of history. It is the sixth sense that en-courages us to hope that entropy is not the final law of the cosmos.

From the religious or spiritual perspective, the modern focus on love-as-intimacy seems narrow, desperate, and claustropho-bic. Love is the impulse and energy that unites us in a com-monwealth of Being, not merely an emotion that binds us to a few individuals in our private sphere.

Listen with fresh ears, if you can, to some of the (slightly revised) claims of Saint Paul's most famous hymn to love: If I speak eloquently and accurately, but have not love, I am nothing but a windbag. And if I have all scientific and predictive powers and understand all mysteries and knowledge, and if I have all faith and technological know-how and can control the environment, but have not love, I am nothing. . . . Love never ends . . . but our knowledge is flawed, and our capacity to predict is imperfect. . . . Our concepts give us only a glimpse of a reflection of the surface of reality, but in love we see face to face. Now I know in part, but when I finally love without reservation, I shall understand fully, even as I have been fully understood. So faith, hope, and love abide, these three; but the greatest of these is love.

How do we make sense out of these claims?

Soundings:
Echoes of the Religious Imagination

What does it mean to speak about God loving us, or about our loving God, or about love being the unifying and creative power of the universe? The moment we depart from the most naïve notion of God—as a superhuman person in the sky, a giant father or an encompassing mother—the word *love* ceases to have any familiar meaning. How do we reinterpret love to make it apply to our least mythological concepts of God as the ground of our being, or the self-surpassing surpasser of all, or Being-Becoming-Itself?

I confess that, although I have been a lifelong candidate for love and a spiritual aspirant, I fall short of being a man of settled faith. I find myself unable either to negotiate the great leap or to abandon the possibility of faith. Both my critical mind and the perennial tragedy of human history keep me from being able to trust easily in the ultimate triumph of love. Nevertheless, I remain poised at the brink, listening to the voices of the religious imagination that echo throughout the abyss. I do not dismiss the possibilities and promises, nor do I discard the wisdom of the great mystical traditions.

My practice in these matters is to ponder, explore, play, imagine, and remain open. I approach the great classical accounts of mystical experience with empathy, allowing them to speak to me, trying to feel what it is like to live within such beliefs.

My method is like that of a sailor who uses a sounding line to probe the fathoms beneath his boat, or a seismologist who sets off small charges of dynamite that send shock waves deep into the earth and that echo back from the region of the tectonic plates. I use certain deep experiences to take soundings of the contours that lie beneath the surface of "normal," superficial consciousness. I invite you to join me in this exploration of the great mystery in which we are all involved.

SOUNDING 1: *Playing with Worldviews*

Humans are not only biomythic but biometaphysical animals. We are forced by our restless consciousness and by the inherent limitations of our knowledge to assemble a worldview the way a child draws a picture, by using lines to connect dots on a page. Each of us takes certain fragments of experience and makes them the key to understanding the whole.

Every worldview, or religious vision, is a kind of thought experiment in cosmic empathy in which we try to imagine our way into the ungraspable totality. Metaphysics is a game played in the subjunctive. "Let's suppose that . . ." "What if we assume that . . ." "Imagine that . . ."

If we extrapolate from the experience of thinking, we may conclude that reality is a form of consciousness or mind. If we extrapolate from the experience of fabrication, we may conclude that we live in a world created by a divine craftsman. If we extrapolate from the experience of organisms, we may conclude that the world is a living being—Gaia. If we extrapolate from the existential experience of plague, war, and death, or the more abstract knowledge of the decay of radioactive particles, we may conclude that the world is a system of energy in a state of devolution. Any pivotal experience may provide us a key analogy from which to construct a worldview.

We have a choice between many metaphysical stories about the nature and destiny of life. But the radical choice we face is between a vision of a dead-end material universe in which life has emerged by accident, evolved by chance, and is fated to destruction, and a vision of an infinitely inventive cosmos that is continually evolving in complexity of form, pattern, hierarchy, differentiation, and ever more conscious and compassionate beings.

Sounding 2: *Imagining a Dead-End Universe*

The dark vision of the modern materialist hero rests on two pillars—the notion that entropy is the governing law of all being, and the assumption that death is the ultimate human destiny.

Ever since science and technology replaced religion as our governing cultural activity, the source of our values and meaning, we have viewed the universe as a system that is governed by entropy—the second law of thermodynamics. Within limits, matter is evolving—complex hierarchies are created from simpler elements—but all that rises must fall. The sons and daughters of earth and the suns of heaven, all things brave and beautiful, last only a moment before they return to dust. In the dictionary definition of *entropy* we read the modern judgment about the nature and destiny of all reality: "Entropy—the ultimate state reached in the degradation of the matter and energy of the universe: state of inert uniformity of component elements: absence of form, pattern, hierarchy or differentiation: the general trend of the universe toward death and disorder."

When a single life is projected against the background of this metaphysical vision, the result is either despair or heroic resignation and rebellion. I know of nobody who has articulated this dark vision more clearly than Bertrand Russell in *A Free Man's Worship*:

> Brief and powerless is man's life; on him and all his race the slow, sure doom falls pitiless and dark. Blind to good and evil, reckless of destruction, omnipotent matter rolls on its relentless way; for man, condemned today to lose his dearest, tomorrow himself to pass through the gate of darkness, it remains only to cherish, ere yet the blow fall, the lofty thoughts that ennoble his little day; disdaining the coward terrors of the slave of Fate, to worship at the shrine that his own hands have built; undismayed by the empire of chance, to preserve a mind free from the wanton tyranny that rules his outward life; proudly defiant of the irresistible forces that tolerate, for a moment, his knowledge and his condemnation, to sustain, alone, a weary but unyielding Atlas, the world that his own ideals have fashioned despite the trampling march of unconscious power.

Saul Bellow's *Herzog* carries the dark vision to its final, existential conclusion:

> What is the philosophy of this generation? Not that God is dead, that period has passed long ago. Perhaps it should be stated death is God. This generation thinks—and this is its thought of thoughts—that nothing faithful, vulnerable, fragile can be durable or have any true power. Death waits for these things as a cement floor waits for a dropping light bulb.

If Russell and Bellow are right, I stand alone in a dying universe, and my life becomes a problem in search of a solution.

SOUNDING 3: *Imagining Inexhaustible Creation*

When we take our stand within the pivotal experience of love, we pass through the looking glass into a world where everything is seen and valued differently.

The lover's perspective on life is binocular rather than monocular, plural rather than singular, communal rather than individual. From within an experience of life in which the "we" is as real as "I," the lover sees a world in which communion is as much a fact as isolation, creation is the Siamese twin of destruction, and the evolution of complexity is the flip side of entropy.

If entropy is the second law of thermodynamics, then continuous evolution is the first law of amourdynamics. Matter and energy conspire to create an inexhaustibly renewable cosmos of continually evolving complexity of form, pattern, hierarchy, and differentiation and of ever more conscious and compassionate beings.

In love we discover something that is inexhaustible.

Loving is like digging a hole at the water's edge on the beach—the more you dig, the more the ocean seeps into your small puddle. The most common testimony of advanced practitioners of the art of love is that love dispels (the illusion of) scarcity. The more you give, the more you have. As our capacity to love expands, we discover at the center of our self an unlimited resource. Love is a win-win game.

When the metaphor of "power" becomes the organizing principle of our psyche and of morality, economics, and politics, we create a worldview governed by the threat of scarcity and a way of life dominated by competition, a zero-sum game in which some win at the expense of others.

The philosophy of love creates complexity; the philosophy of power destroys complexity.

The entropic vision conceptualizes the universe as a closed energy system in the process of being reduced to inert uniformity of component elements. As a general rule, when power, force, or energy becomes the central organizing metaphor and concern in any system—natural, psychological, interpersonal, corporate, or political—its tendency is to reduce rather than enhance complexity and creativity. For example, a tyrannical leader exerts power in an effort to reduce people to conforming units that can be controlled. All totalitarian relationships try to destroy the natural diversity of the human community in order to produce an anthill society in which people are interchangeable, standardized units that can be controlled. The result is inevitably a conforming mass that lacks color, spirit, or creativity. Witness the inert uniformity, artistic sterility, and cultural poverty that have resulted from the recent tyrannical regimes in the USSR, China, and North Korea. In a similar way a dominating parent stunts the creativity of the child.

It is the nature of love to rejoice in complexity. When we care for others, we release them from the pressure to conform to our notions of what they should do and be and encourage them to follow their own vision. As Howard Thurman—professor of spiritual resources and disciplines, mystic, friend—frequently said to me: "Follow the grain in your own wood." It is precisely the unique, special, and unrepeatable Being of the beloved that inspires desire and devotion. A good parent encourages a child to develop its unique gifts and delights in its growing independence. All the everyday litanies of love celebrate the idiosyncratic and unique: "When they made Jim, they threw away the pattern." "You aren't like anybody I've ever known before." "She's one of a kind." "You're special."

Love initiates us into an expanding universe.

The impulse to desire, know, and care that begins at the breast drives us into ever more inclusive concentric circles—from mother to father, to family, to neighbor, to community, to the "enemy," to the encompassing world. Love seeks to expand, to include whatever becomes known. In the course of a lifetime, egocentric loving of "me and mine" proceeds to social caring about "us" (but not "them") and leads in the end to compassion for all sentient beings. Like a universal solvent, love keeps dissolving boundaries and containers.

It is because love is by nature expansive that it is eventually linked with the demand for justice. Once I begin to be moved by compassion, I will inevitably become concerned with the welfare of an ever widening circle of fellow-creatures. In this way love may give our lives an increasing richness of meaning, an expanded identity, but it does not leave us content, satisfied, and secure. If we are not troubled by what is happening to our kindred on the mean streets of Nigeria, Nicaragua, and New York, it is only because we refuse to allow our compassion to expand beyond the range of our potency.

SOUNDING 4: *And Death Shall Have No Dominion*

The language of love is saturated with the promise of transcending the normal limits of time and space. By its own testimony, love doesn't belong to the realm of origins and endings. It lives in the timeless dimension of eternity, of always and forever, in which there is no past or future. As the poet Rumi said: "Lovers don't finally meet somewhere. They're in each other all along." Most of us have said to someone we have come to love, "It seems as if I have known you forever." And love songs promise: "I'll be loving you always." "The Rockies may tumble . . . but, oh my dear, our love is here to stay."

Even if we assume that much of this is romantic hyperbole, it is hard to dismiss lightly the claim of the world-weary poet of Ecclesiastes that "love is strong as death." A scene in Norman McLean's autobiographical story *A River Runs Through It* articulates the experience as elegantly and simply as anything I know. After a disagreement, Norman and his wife, Jessie, stand in a doorway, kiss, and make up. "Without interrupting each other, we both said at the same time, 'Let's never get out of touch with each other.' And we never have, although her death has come between us."

It is this deeply experienced but impossible-to-explain negation of the finality of death that led Gabriel Marcel to say that the beloved is, in some incomprehensible way, indestructible and eternal. A character in one of Marcel's plays says that to love another is to affirm, "Thou, at least, thou shalt not die." Within love there is a demand for perenniality, an apprehension that the other is and that nothing can destroy what truly is. It is only in love that the assurance is given to us that something resists the acids of time and abides even if all else passes away.

Following the death of a parent, child, friend, or lover, something strange happens to us that escapes our categories of understanding and is difficult to speak about with any clarity. To the bereaved it is *as if* the beloved continues to be mysteriously present. My father, who has been dead for thirty-two years, remains an active presence, with whom I have a continuing relationship. Some would say that my father's spirit exists in a nonmaterial realm and is literally present to me. But because my mind cannot quite admit such a metaphysic, I merely say that "he appears regularly in my fantasies, my dreams, and my imagination."

It is difficult to know exactly what conclusions to draw from our sense that in loving we touch something inexhaustible, ever expansive, creative, complexifying, and deathless. We simply do not have any satisfactory intellectual needles upon which to knit these subtle experiences. It seems cynical to dismiss them as purely subjective, wishful-thinking, comforting illusions. And it seems naïve to claim that they are proof-positive that love makes the world go 'round.

SOUNDING 5: *Micro-Macrocosmic Love*

Every religious tradition has a repertoire of thought experiments and spiritual disciplines that help us imagine and feel what it would be like to live within a goodly or Godly cosmos. Prayer, for instance, is a way of placing ourselves in relationship to an ultimate reality that we assume is responsive to our loving concerns. "Almighty and most merciful God, unto whom all hearts are open, all desires known . . ."

A Buddhist meditation, which I have adapted and expanded, invites us to experience our life within a love-governed world.

• Imagine you are lying warm and secure within the arms of your (ideal) mother. Imagine the love you see in her eyes and the pleasure you feel in her embrace. Imagine the harmony of your synchronized breathing, your hearts beating in the same rhythm. Imagine how your bodies melt, and you flow together to become a single being, a motherandchild.

• Now, make a leap of faith and dare to imagine that the feeling of unity and compassion you feel in your mother's arms is a revelation of the nature of the deepest creative power of the universe.

• When you have placed yourself within the harmony, melting, adoration, appreciation, and pleasure of your most full-hearted moment of love, imagine how your boundaries were expanded in such moments. Think about the great mythic questions from within this perspective. Who are you? What is real? What is illusion? Who is your neighbor? Who is your enemy? Whom can you love? For what may you hope? What ought you to do? What work is worth doing? What is possible? Think about the priorities of your life, your work, your plans for the future not as an individual but as a microcosmic-macrocosmic lover.

This meditation points to the radical transformation of our identity that love creates when we consider it not as a mere feeling but as a gateway into a worldview. Because it destroys our egocentric perspective, love changes our sense of who we are, our values and moral priorities.

• Imagine that those persons you usually ignore or exile from your concern—the dispossessed, powerless, poor, homeless, foreigners, criminals, enemies, the sick and dying, and so on—are your neighbors and kin. Seen in this light, any stranger may become as precious to you as your most intimate loved one.
• Imagine that every living being, from a bouncing baby to an indigo bunting, is equally an expression of the life-force and the love-force. Seen in this light, the life of every sentient being may become as precious as your life is to you.

Once we consider the world from within the feeling and sense of reality that we have for our mothers, fathers, wives, husbands, lovers, children, friends, we are forced to live in a state of moral tension. Love creates a moral paradox: Our capacity to care for others is limited, yet the needs of a multitude of suffering beings place an infinite demand on us. Compassion initiates us into a tragic world in which we must somehow be content with the charity and good works we can accomplish

and be discontent with our moral failure in not accomplishing
more.

SOUNDING 6: *The Vast and Intimate Cosmos*

The mystical tradition does not pretend to offer any objective, theoretical, verifiable knowledge *about* a distant God beyond time or space. What it offers is a testimony to an
experience of intimacy *with* a sacred reality that is inseparable
both from the self and from the surrounding world.

Without such an experience, we are left to contemplate the
empty heavens. Here let Blaise Pascal, the seventeenth-century
French philosopher and scientist, speak for us:

> When I consider the short extent of my life, swallowed up
> in the eternity of before and after, the small space that I
> fill or even see, engulfed in the infinite immensity of
> spaces unknown to me and which know me not, I am
> terrified and astounded to find myself here and not there.
> For there is no reason why it should be here, not there,
> why now rather than at another time.

We, in more recent times, have grown used to Carl Sagan,
in the television series *Cosmos*, repeating with liturgical regularity how the Earth is only "a pale blue dot" among "billions
and billions of stars," "a very small stage in a vast cosmic
arena."

By contrast, the psalmists of the Old Testament constantly
celebrated the cosmos not as a neutral or alien environment
but as an arena of God's action and care: "The heavens are
telling the glory of God; and the firmament proclaims his hand-
iwork."

Perhaps the strongest biblical statement of the experience of mystical intimacy with God is found in Psalm 139. Here the Psalmist seeks God not in the outer world but in the inmost reaches of the self.

> O Lord, thou hast searched me and known me! Thou knowest when I sit down and when I rise up; Thou discernest my thoughts from afar. Thou searchest out my path and my lying down, and are acquainted with all my ways. . . . For Thou didst form my inward parts, Thou didst knit me together in my mother's womb. . . . Thou knowest me right well; my frame was not hidden from Thee, when I was being made in secret, intricately wrought in the depths of the earth. Thine eyes beheld my substance, yet being imperfect; and in Thy book all my members were written, which in continuance were fashioned, when as yet there was none of them.

The Psalmist's reaction to experiencing himself as a creature who was intended and in-formed throughout the entire process of evolution and who is known in every atom of his being is a feeling of the awe-ful and marvelous inescapability of God: "Whither shall I go from Thy spirit, or whither shall I flee from Thy presence? If I ascend to heaven, Thou art there. If I make my bed in Hell, Thou art there. . . . If I say, 'Surely the darkness will cover me' . . . even the darkness is not dark to Thee." Although he can address God and celebrate being a creature ("I will praise Thee, for I am fearfully and wonderfully made, marvelous are Thy works and that my soul knows right well"), he knows that he remains theologically ignorant. The carnal intimacy and assurance he experiences does not add up to any claim to comprehend God. "Such knowledge is too wonderful for me; it is high, I cannot attain it."

The religious vision provides a framework that makes intelligible the veiled insight, with which we began our quest, that love is the solution to the problem of meaning. If we are known, encompassed, intended by God, then love is not just an emotion, a chemical impulse, or a social bond but is "the ontological drive toward the reunion of the separated," as Paul Tillich said. When we love deeply, we are reunited with the source of our being, and we find our identity and meaning as part of the connective tissue that holds the network of being together, as participants in the great unfolding drama that is the created and creating cosmos.

One of the major challenges each of us faces is to find a way to recover that sense of trust and security we (ideally) experienced in our parents' arms. As we are cast out of the Eden of childhood, we fall into a world ruled by fear, greed, and delusion in which it seems unsafe to trust. The religious affirmation "God is love" offers a path to "second innocence," a return to the mythic state of basic trust, by encouraging us to take the risk of loving even in the presence of tragedy.

SOUNDING 7: Eros *and Human Destiny*

The mystical tradition envisions the human and divine *eros* as inseparable. It sometimes goes so far as to suggest that sexual desire itself may become a royal path to spiritual realization.

Institutional religion, with its focus on miracle, mystery, and authority, usually encourages the faithful to rise above the temptations of the flesh, to abandon the lower desires of the body and cultivate the higher desires of the spirit.

But if we rummage beneath the orthodox facades, we discover that every major religious tradition has a mystical, esoteric teaching that uses sexuality as a means to heighten spiritual awareness. And vice versa! The Song of Solomon, the Taoist pillow books, the sexual disciplines of Tantra, the erotic statuary of the Hindu temple at Kajaraho, the outrageous tales of the rogue Buddhist saint Drugpa Kinley, the sexual imagery of the Christian mystics from Saint Catherine to William Blake, all suggest something that is as scandalous to the pious believer as it is to the secular nonbeliever: Sexual intimacy may be cultivated so that it becomes a sacramental experience.

• Imagine that your most wholehearted sexual intimacy is a sacramental pleasure in which you are reenacting and participating in the sacred process of cosmic creation. When you make love, you are co-creating history.

• Imagine sexual desire as a sacred vocation that calls you into the fullness of being.

When we dedicate ourselves to learn and practice all of the elements of love, all our relationships become sacred. Whenever we truly meet another person, we may celebrate the incarnation of love, experience the spirit becoming flesh, feel time moving on the edge of eternity, dwell on consecrated ground.

Discovering a pathway to the sacred creativity of Being through our sexual longings is only a special case of discovering that the essential longing that animates human consciousness is a mark of the immanence of the Divine Spirit.

Humans are the only insatiable animals. When our every biological, psychological, and sociological need is satisfied, we are still driven by a desire that has no identifiable object. We are creatures of longing. What we call the human "spirit" is this hunger that is never satisfied. The arrows, the *eros,* of our longing never hit their final target. Our quest for an unimaginable fulfillment is built into our DNA.

One possible explanation: When the cerebral cortex evolved, humans became both conscious and self-conscious. And because we are self-observing, symbol-using animals, we imagine future goods and invent ideals that always lie beyond our reach. This imagining, as Albert Camus said, condemns us to absurdity because we long for beauty, justice, and kindness in a world where there will always be ugliness, injustice, and cruelty. Or as Jean-Paul Sartre said, our insatiable hunger for an impossible fulfillment is not a sign that we are creatures of spirit but rather a "useless passion." An evolutionary explanation of human yearning suggests that at the moment we became self-conscious and human, we fell from the paradise of innocence and became neurotic animals destined for unhappiness.

Perhaps, as Walt Whitman suggested, we should

> *turn and live with animals, they are so placid and self-*
> *contain'd . . .*
> *They do not sweat and whine about their condition,*
> *They do not lie awake in the dark and weep for their sins,*
> *They do not make me sick discussing their duty to God,*
> *Not one is dissatisfied.*

Another explanation: The mystical vision emerges from an effort to understand the difference between the experience of self as ego and the experience of self as spirit by peeling away layer after layer of superficial wants and needs until we reach the bedrock of desire—the ontological longing. When every material desire is satiated, there remains a yearning, a drive toward an unforeseeable fulfillment that is inseparable from human consciousness. The mystical claim is that this yearning is a token of our true identity, a promise of our ultimate destiny, a redolence of a rose now only in bud.

• Imagine that your yearning for fulfillment is the immanence of the divine presence, Spirit inspiring spirit, Brahman within Atman.

• Imagine that the deepest moving force within you is the desire to be reunited with the creative source from whom your life and all blessings flow and to whom you are destined to return—that God whom we call by ten thousand names.

• Imagine that your driving *eros* is governed by your *telos* (goal, destiny, metaphysical DNA). Or as Augustine said, "Oh God, Thou hast made us for Thyself, and our hearts are restless until they rest in Thee."

• Imagine that your fundamental dissatisfaction is a form of divine discontent, not a mark of your failure or a consequence of the absurdity of life.

• Imagine that your nostalgia for fulfillment is a kind of memory of the future, an expectation of returning to a homeland you inhabited in the mythic once-upon-a-time.

• Imagine your life is a love story in process. You are a creature driven by a mysterious purposiveness that pervades every cell of your body and energizes your nervous system, that is inseparable from the drive toward comprehension you call your mind and the urge toward com-passion you call your heart or spirit. *Eros* is the force that weaves the strands of your DNA to create a future that transcends every past, your questing consciousness, your *élan vital*, your *chi*, your life energy. You are essentially an erotic creature.

• Imagine your brief life is encompassed within a universe that seems to yearn its way (evolve) toward an unimaginable cosmic fulfillment. As Saint Paul suggested, the cosmos is pregnant, and we exist in the last days before it gives birth. The *eros* that informs your being is interior to the Cosmic Eros—the unifying, evolving Totality of what was, is, and will be.

In the end, the strangest thing about humankind is not that we are pragmatic creatures made of the same whirling atoms and unstable compounds as stones and stars. It is that we are constructed of the stuff of poetry and dreams. As Norman O. Brown says in his great paean *Love's Body*: "The reality of the body is not given . . . ; the body is . . . to be built not with hands but by the spirit; Man makes Himself, his own body, in the symbolic freedom of the imagination. The Eternal Body of Man is the Imagination." Nowhere do we experience this intoxicating freedom, this divine power to create, so certainly as in the loving imagination. In trusting the images and echoes that arise out of our deepest experiences of belonging and communion, we discover, even as we fail again and again, that the way of love sustains the faith and hope that give abiding meaning to human life.

LOVE ALONE
ITS VIGIL KEEPING

❧

It is time to end. And I've always had trouble with endings. I want to go on and on polishing and improving, making this work, this life, more beautiful.

When I was a child, I ended each day with prayer. Dutifully I confessed my sins, asked for forgiveness, and beseeched God to help me be better, keep me safe, and grant me eternal life. Mostly the answer to my prayers was not blessed assurance but an acute awareness of my failure to love and a restless striving for impossible perfection.

In due course, I rebelled against the guilt-provoking dogmas, disciplines, and authorities of evangelical Protestantism and crafted my own homemade spiritual practice that made a virtue of questioning and a comfort of not knowing. But when my children came along, I didn't know what to do about their "religious" education. I didn't have a set of answers or a creed, and yet I wanted to give them some sense of the authentic challenge and abiding comfort that is present in all the great religious traditions. Finally I settled on a nightly ritual in which I asked them to remember and give thanks for the blessings of the day. And then each night for thousands of nights, I eased them into sleep by singing the ancient lullaby.

Sleep, my child,
And peace attend thee
All through the night.
Guardian angels
God will send thee
All through the night.
Soft the drowsy
Hours are creeping,
Hill and dale
In slumber steeping;
Love alone
Its vigil keeping
All through the night

It's getting on toward dusk now, and the hours remaining before nightfall pass all too rapidly, and I find myself singing the old lullaby again—this time to myself. At long last I have a modicum of faith that it is love alone that keeps the vigil in dark times. The inheritors of the Enlightenment, the servants of the modern god Progress, would like us to believe that peace and prosperity are just an invention away. But the excessive light of high noon creates a mirage. At the moment our spiritual horizon is filled with cheap optimism—vague visions of utopia that will be ushered in by technological messiahs and market economies. Meanwhile, global poverty grows, ecocide escalates, and genocide is back in fashion. Any realistic analysis of the state of the world must conclude that we live in troubled times and are not likely to be healed by Progress.

The vigil that love keeps in the perennial darkness of human history does not give us a vision of triumph or a promise of perfection. The great clarity it offers is the certain knowledge that we are sundered, dismembered, alienated from the totality to which we belong ("sinners," in the old religious language)—

and the hope, which is inseparable from prayer, that what has been dismembered can be remembered. Our longing to be re-united with our self, our parents, our children, our lovers, our neighbors, our animal familiars, is at once a token of our exile and our citizenship in a commonwealth of Beings. And prayer is nothing more or less than remembering and re-minding ourselves to participate joyously in that community within which we live and move and have our being.

To love, to hope, to pray is to wager that communion rather than isolation is the ultimate fact that governs human destiny, and to wait—all through the night.

ABOUT THE AUTHOR

Sam Keen holds an S.T.B. and a Th.M. from Harvard Divinity School and a Ph.D. in philosophy of religion from Princeton University. He was for many years a consulting editor of *Psychology Today* and is the author of twelve previous books, including *Faces of the Enemy*, *To a Dancing God*, *Hymns to an Unknown God*, and the *New York Times* bestseller, *Fire in the Belly*.